EARLY CHILDHOOD ACTIVITIES

A Treasury of Ideas from Worldwide Sources

by

Elaine Commins

Cover Design by William Prankard

HUMANICS LIMITED
P.O. Box 7447
Atlanta, Georgia 30309

Library of Congress Card Catalog Number: 81-83051
PRINTED IN THE UNITED STATES OF AMERICA
ISBN 0-89334-066-9

Jean Piaget said, "Active experience with solid objects form the raw material that is later organized into knowledge."

The experiences and activities that are offered in this book reflect a commitment to this philosophy.

TABLE OF CONTENTS

PREFACE

Early childhood education is vitally important to the welfare of young children. It is therefore essential that teachers and parents of young children have at their disposal the best activities from every available source for use in the classroom and home. Included here are ideas from traditional schools, Montessori schools, the British Infant schools, Head Start programs and experimental classrooms. In addition, this book contains the suggestions of noted educators and ideas taken from conventions, conferences, kits and workshops. Activities from seven subjects are presented: art, language arts, mathematics, music, physical education, science and social studies. This comprehensive survey of early childhood activities will provide teachers and parents with ready access to hundreds of select ideas from teaching systems worldwide.

Art has no nationality. It can be adapted from any teaching system to fit into another; it can be adjusted to suit any child. It is the creative mainstay of early childhood education.

With the understanding that performance is infinitely more valuable than the end product, teachers should encourage honest and innovative efforts without pressuring students to attain specific results. The child who becomes totally absorbed in the process of creating often finds self-satisfaction in terms of emotional growth as well as artistic rewards. This self-satisfaction in turn has a positive affect on the total learning environment.

The most important single element in a successful art program is variety. By offering a different activity each day, the teacher insures that children will approach the art table eagerly and with a sense of anticipation. Included in this volume are high interest projects and crafts designed specifically to appeal to children and to match their developmental level.

A. PAINTING AND COLORING

Easel Painting

The art table and one easel should be sufficient for the average classroom. Prepare the easels with a variety of clean, bold colors each day. On occasion, substitute pastels for variety.

The least expensive type of paint seems to be powdered tempera that is mixed with water. For economy, it is best to only half fill the paint cups. Save leftover paint by removing the brushes and covering each paint container tightly.

Newsprint or other inexpensive paper is adequate for daily use. Use the classified section of the newspaper or wallpaper samples for novel substitutes. Long handled brushes, 1/4", 1/2" or 1" in size, are recommended for small children.

The only instructions that experts advise giving children at the easel are to keep each brush in its own color and to wipe brushes on the side of the paint container to prevent excessive dripping.

Easel Painting With One Color

Using a single color, prepare graduated shades of the paint with black and white paint. Line the jars of the various shades of paint in order from darkest to palest at the easel.

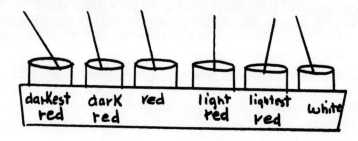

Painting at Tables With Odd-Sized Paper

Provide unusual sizes and shapes of paper for children to paint. Suggested shapes are:
    Long paper (suggests buildings or trains)
    Square paper
    Round paper
    Wide paper
    Free shaped paper that is torn around the edges

Topics for Painting

Franz Cizek, founder of the Juvenile Art Class in Vienna, Austria, in 1897 established a basic system of revolutionary techniques which remain valid today. Usually the teacher or the students suggest a topic and the class engages in a descriptive and colorful conversation which helps each child create mental word pictures.

After this verbal motivation, the teacher provides students with pencils, paints and crayons. Give the students large sheets of paper (12" x 18"). Have the children draw the picture first with pencil and then color it. The only other instruction to give the children is that they draw large figures. Some suggestions for topics are:
    Self-portraits
    Me and my family
    My house
    My doll (pet, toy, etc.)
    I am running (jumping, swimming, fishing, riding, eating, swinging, falling, bathing, etc.)
    I visit Santa Claus (grandmother, the doctor, etc.)
    I see a gigantic rainbow.
    The balloon man comes to my street.
    The ice cream man comes to my street.
    The flower lady
    A big city (farm, zoo, circus, park, train station, etc.)
    I land on the moon (a star, another planet)
    Circus clowns
    Space man
    Faces (large portraits)
    I go to the beach (the mountains, the desert, a lake, etc.)
    Paint a happy picture (a sad picture)

Paint a summer picture (winter, spring, autumn)
Paint what you think is out the window
Paint a dream
Paint the Indians who used to live here
Paint an explosion in a paint factory
Paint a fairy (monster, ghost, giant, witch, etc.)
Paint another child in the class[1]

Skating On Paper

Lowenfeld and Brittain originated this activity and it had been used successfully in many classes.[2]

Material: Manila paper
          Dark felt tipped marker
          Crayons

Method: Instruct children to pretend their marker is a skate which they glide over the paper. They then color in the design they've created with crayons.

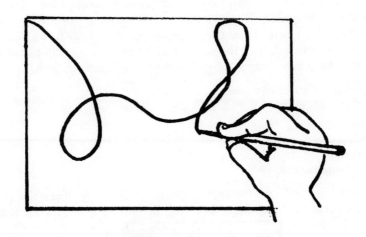

Wax Relief Painting

Materials: Manila paper
           Wax candles or paraffin
           Paint brushes
           Watery tempera paint

Method: Children draw a design on their paper with a candle or paraffin, then paint the entire surface over with the tempera. The paint will not adhere to the waxed surface and the wax picture will emerge.

---

[1]From *Child Art* by Wilhem Viola. Copyright © 1944 by Bennett Publishing Company. Used with permission.

[2]*Creative and Mental Growth,* Fifth Edition, by Viktor Lowenfield and W. Lambert Brittain. Copyright © 1970 MacMillan Publishing Co., Inc.

Wax Relief Seascapes

Materials: Manila paper
Pencils
Crayons
Paint brushes
Watery blue tempera paint

Method: Children use pencils to draw things that they think they might find under the surface of the ocean such as fish, plants, turtles, seahorses, octopuses, crabs, shells, submarines, etc. When the drawing is finished, the children color heavily with crayons *only* the objects they've drawn. Then they wash over the entire surface with the thin blue tempera.

Wax Relief Paintings of the Seasons

Materials: Manila paper or dark construction paper
Crayons
Pencils
Brushes
Watery tempera paint

Method: Have the children draw fall scenes (falling leaves, birds flying south, jack-o-lanterns, turkeys, etc.); winter scenes (on dark construction paper) (snow, Christmas trees, etc.); spring scenes (flowers, butterflies, bees, kites, etc.); and summer scenes (firecrackers, sailboats, beaches, etc.) in pencil. Then the children color in heavily with crayon the objects they've drawn and wash over the surface with tempera. For fall pictures, use an orange or red paint; for winter, white; for spring, green; for summer, blue.

Wax Relief Design Using Circles and Lines

Materials: 9" x 12" manilla paper
Crayons
Rulers
Various sized jar lids
Watery tempera paint

Method: Children outline circles and straight lines on paper. They then color parts of the design heavily with crayons. Then they wash over the entire paper with a pale tinted tempera.

Sponge painting

Materials: Sponges cut into small shapes
Bowls of different colored tempera paint
Paper
Clothspins to hold the sponges with, if desired

Method: Place several bowls of tempera paint on the art table along with a number of sponges. The child dips the sponge into the paint, rubs off excess paint on the edge of the bowl and dabs the sponge on the paper to make a design.

Sponge Painting Around Stencils

Materials: Sponges cut into small shapes
Bowls of different colored tempera paint
Paper
Clothespins to hold the sponges with, if desired
Stencils of animals, trees, etc.

Method: Place a stencil on the center of the child's paper and have him sponge paint around it.

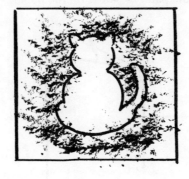

Powdered Tempera Pictures

Materials: Small bowls of tempera paint in powder form
Brushes
Bowls of water
Paper

Method: Children first dip their brushes into the water, then into the powdered paint. They then apply their brushes to the paper to make a picture.

Wet Paper Pictures

Materials: A large pan of water (such as a plastic dish pan)
Brushes
Paint
Felt markers (optional)

Method: Children immerse their sheets of paper in water, than load a brush with paint and touch it to the paper at different points. Be sure the children use a different brush for each color. The paint will blend. If desired, after the paper is dry, the children may outline the areas of color with a felt marker.

Crazy Colors

Materials: Manila paper
Pencils
Paint or crayons

Method: Children draw pictures on their paper with pencil. They then paint each object an unnatural color (for example, green sun, blue tree, purple person, etc.)

String Painting

Materials: Paper
  String (10" or 12" long)
  Paint in bowls

Method: The children fold their papers in half. They dip one end of their string in paint and put the painted end inside the folded paper. They then close the paper, press it gently, and pull the string out, allowing the paint to smear on the paper.

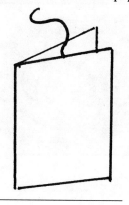

Blowing Paint

Materials: Straws
  2 or 3 different colors of paint in bowls
  Paper or paper plates

Method: Drop a small glob of paint on the child's paper. You may want to use paper plates since they have a built-in border. The chld then blows the paint with a straw to make a design. He can repeat the process if he wants to add more or a different color to the picture.

Bubble Paintings

Materials: Straws
  Tempera paint mixed with liquid detergent
  Paper

Method: Mix the paint and soap in bowls and let the children take turns blowing bubbles with their straws. Then have the children place their papers on the bubbles so that the bubbles "print" a pattern on the paper. Let the children repeat the procedure several times using the same or a different colored paint so that other areas of the paper can be "painted" by the bubbles.

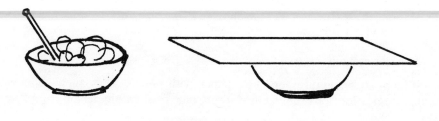

8

Window Paintings

Materials: Tempera paint
          Brushes
          Any available window

Method: The teacher paints a simple outline of a snowman, tree, flower, etc. on the window. Children fill in the outline with paint. You will probably want to use a dropcloth.

Stained Glass Paintings

Materials: Tracing paper
          Tempera paint
          Black felt markers
          Colored construction paper

Method: The teacher cuts out frames from construction paper in advance. Have the children paint designs on the tracing paper. Make sure the children use lots of bright colors and fill up the entire paper with paint. Then staple the paintings to the frames. After the pictures have dried, the children may outline areas of color with black markers to indicate "leaded" areas.

Seasonal Paintings

Materials: Paper
          Brushes
          Paint

Method: Prepare two tables. One will be for summer pictures and will be supplied with paint in warm colors: red, yellow and orange. The second table will be for winter pictures and will be supplied with cool colors: blue, green and purple. Have the children paint pictures at both tables. Give an art show and have the children decide which paintings belong in the winter gallery and which belong in the summer gallery.

Spatter Painting on the Floor

Materials: Paint
          Stiff bristle brushes such as toothbrushes, vegetables brushes, etc.
          Newspaper to cover the surrounding floor
          18" × 12" manilla paper
          Sticks or pencils
          Stencils (optional)

Method: Spread newspaper out generously over the portion of the floor to be used. Have the children don smocks. They put their papers on the newspaper, dip their brushes into thin tempera paint, and draw a stick or pencil over the brush to make the paint spatter. If desired, put a stencil on the paper.

Body Portraits

Materials: Roll of 36" wide wrapping paper
          Felt marking pens
          Paint

Method: The teacher outlines each child's silhouette as he or she lies on the paper on the floor. Leaving the paper on the floor, the children paint their own pictures.

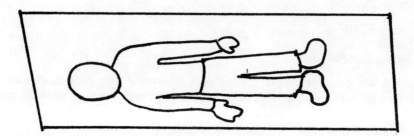

Cooperative Portrait

Materials: Roll of 36" wide wrapping paper
           Felt marking pen
           Paint

Method: In conjunction with a holiday or special event the children paint a life-sized portrait, similar to the body portrait described above, of an astronaut, clown, Christopher Columbus, Abraham Lincoln, etc. Using a child as a model, the teacher traces an outline of a person on the paper. The teacher then alters the picture to add details so that it resembles a specific person. For instance, add a stove-pipe hat if your subject is Abraham Lincoln. Clearly define areas such as the subject's shoes, pants, hat, scarf, belt, shirt, etc. Then allow each child to paint one section.

Bouquets

Materials: Paper
           Paint
           Crayons
           Brushes

Method: Have the children color large dark dots on their papers with crayons. They then dip a brush in paint and paint petals around each dot. An easy method is to paint outward from each dot with a single stroke.

Montessori Metal Insets

Montessori schools have an activity which seems to be unique with them: the use of metal insets combined with colored pencils. Ten metal insets are offered the children. They are the oval, the triangle, the pentagon, the circle, the ellipse, the square, the quatre-foil, the rectangle, the curvilinear triangle, and the trapezoid.

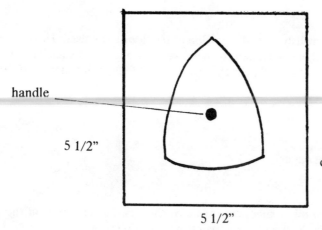

handle

5 1/2"

5 1/2"

Children learn to trace the inset after it is lifted out of the frame. They then learn to trace its outline or stencil.

curvilinear triangle

In the Montessori system, children are introduced to these shapes in stages. In the first stage, they may trace one shape and color it in. They work on small pieces of paper on a coloring tray. After they have begun to learn to hold the pencil properly and color evenly, they may use two shapes. They then also have the option of using one shape in two different ways on their paper.

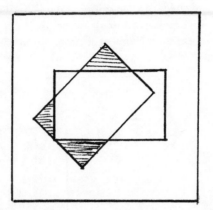

Next, the children may use three shapes or one shape in three different ways. They are gradually introduced to shading and color mixing. The final stage is for the child to create original designs using as many shapes and colors as desired. He may make these designs on large sheets of paper.

Whatever art project Montessori students engage in, they are required to take special care of material and clean up after themselves by washing brushes, wiping up paint spills, returning equipment to its proper place, etc.

Group Painting

Materials: Roll of 36" wide wrapping paper
Paint
Brushes
Masking tape

Method: Tape both ends of a long sheet of the wrapping paper to the floor. Suggest a topic for the painting such as Santa's workshop, animals in the jungle, a flower garden, the street I live on, etc. Let one or two children paint at a time. To avoid spills, put the paint in a soft drink carton.

Zoo Animals

Materials: Paper
Crayons
Yarn
Tape

Method: Give the children a piece of manilla paper on which they are to draw and color an animal or animals. Then punch four holes at the top and four holes at the bottom of each picture for the childre to lace "cages" over the picture with the yarn. Roll tape around the end of the yarn to finish it for ease in lacing the "cage." Tape the yarn in place on the back of the picture when the "cage" is complete.

Finger Painting

Finger painting is a form of painting which combines kinesthetic and small muscle activity. Children should be given aprons to wear and informed that their hands will get dirty. You may wish to demonstrate techniques such as thumb prints, fist prints, knuckle prints and palm prints as well as finger tracings.

Materials: You may use one of the following finger paint recipes:
1. Liquid starch plus powdered tempera
2. Hair setting gel plus powdered tempera
3. Silkscreen mix plus powdered tempera
4. Wallpaper paste made with three parts water, one part wheat paste flour, and coloring
5. For infants, chocolate pudding is a safe substitute for paint.
Commercial finger paint is also available but it tends to be expensive.

Method: The two most widely used methods of finger painting are:

1. Wet the slick side of finger paint paper with a sponge and apply a spoonful of paint. Children then use their hands to form a design.

2. Put a spoonful of finger paint on a formica-topped table. Add water if it is needed. Children then use their hands to form a design on the tabletop. When they have achieved the design they want, the children press a piece of manila paper onto the paint design and lift off a print. This method is a form of printing.

Additional Activities:

1. *Scratch Designs.* Cover the paper with thick tempera. The child uses his fingers and the pointed handle of a brush to scratch a design.

2. *Stencil Tracing.* After the child has finished a finger paint picture and it is dry, the child traces a stencil of an animal or other object on it and cuts it out.

3. Put finished finger paint papers on an easel and have the children fill in the unpainted areas with various colored tempera paint.

4. Have the children beat soap powder and warm water with an egg beater. Add tempera for color and let the children use the mixture as a finger paint.

5. Have the children use two primary colors on one finger paint paper so that they discover the colors' mixing properties.

Trace a butterfly stencil on the paper and cut it out.

Finger Paint Tray

Materials: Plastic tray
           Finger paint

Method: Put blobs of paint in the tray. Use either one or two colors. Let one child at a time make designs in the tray. Let him use the tray for as long as he wants, if possible.

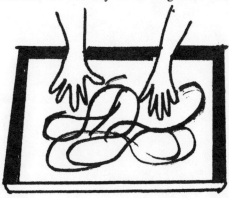

Roll-on Paint Pictures

Materials: Empty roll-on deodorant bottles
        Tempera paint

Method: Clean each bottle thoroughly and fill it with tempera. Let the children create roll-on pictures using the bottles as applicators.

Marble Painting

Materials: Tops of shoe boxes
        Manila, construction or typing paper
        Paint
        Marbles

Method: The child places a sheet of paper in the box lid and spoons a very small amount of paint on the paper. The child then places five or six marbles in the box top and rolls them around by manipulating the box top, making a design with the paint. If desired, he may add another color to the same picture.

B. CRAFTS

Crafts need not be expensive. Scrap material such as pebbles, shells, egg shells, ribbon, felt, string, net, cloth remnants, old wallpaper books, straws, macaroni, paper plates, sequins, buttons, baking cups, sand, bottle caps, etc., can all be used. Children should be encouraged to contribute articles from home such as empty toilet paper rolls, oatmeal containers, egg cartons, tissue boxes, juice cans, coffee tins, old magazines, etc.

1. Paper Crafts

Daisy Chains

Materials: Strips of colored construction paper
                   Paste

Method: Demonstrate how to put paste on the end of one strip of paper and paste it to the other end to form a circle. Slip each strip through a completed ring before pasting it together to form a new ring. Let the children make chains of whatever length they like.

Weaving Paper

This should be considered a preliminary exercise toward weaving loops of cloth on looms.

Materials: Construction paper
                   Strips of various colored paper
                   Scissors
                   Stapler

Method: Each child folds in half a 9" X 12" piece of paper. The teacher draws a straight line 1½" to 2" from and parallel to one of the cut edges. Children cut a series of parallel slits from the folded edge to the teacher's guiding line. The slits will be perpendicular to the guiding line. The children open the papers flat and weave strips in and out of the slits. They begin each strip alternately over and then under the paper. To make it simpler, they may use two colors of strips, alternating them.

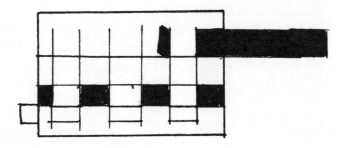

Texture Rubbings

Materials: Paper
                   Crayons
                   Variety of fairly flat objects such as paper clips, pins, corrugated paper, buttons, coins, leaves, etc.

Method: The child selects one object at a time and places a sheet of paper over it. Then, using the long side of a crayon, he or she rubs back and forth on the paper over the object while holding the paper steady with the other hand. Then the child puts another object under a different area of the same paper and repeats the procedure.

Paper Lanterns

Materials: Pieces of 9" × 12" construction paper
Scissors
Stapler

Method: Children fold their papers lengthwise. The teacher draws a guiding line 1½" from one of the open ends. The children cut slits from the folded edge to the line. Staple together the short ends of the paper. Staple a paper handle to the top of the lantern as shown.

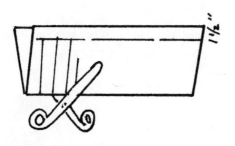 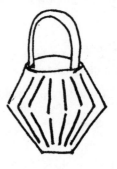

Pasting and Tearing

Materials: Colored construction paper
Paste
Manila paper

Method: Children tear strips from the colored construction paper and paste them on their manila paper in designs of their choice.

Carbon Paper Pictures

Materials: Typing paper
Carbon paper cut to 6" × 9" (half the size of the typing paper)
Pencils
Crayon

Method: Fold the typing paper in half and put a piece of carbon paper inside. Making sure that the dark side of the carbon paper faces down, the children draw on the outside of the typing paper. The children open their papers and color in the designs they have made.

Ironed Pictures

Materials: Waxed paper
An iron
Variety of materials such as leaves, glitter, sequins, crayon shavings, confetti, etc.

Method: Cut each child two pieces of waxed paper. Each child lays out a design using the scrap materials on one sheet of paper. He then covers the first sheet with another sheet of waxed paper of equal size and then either he or the teacher irons the two sheets together. Close teacher supervision of this activity is essential.

Blotter Paper Pictures

Materials: White blotter paper cut to 6" × 9"
Thin tempera paint
Small paint brushes
Construction paper (optional)

Method: Children paint designs on their blotters. If desired, mount the finished product on construction paper.

Snowflakes

Materials: Typing paper
Scissors
Some type of colored paper (either cellophane, tissue paper, or construction paper) to be used as a background.

Method: The teacher traces a large circle on each piece of typing paper. Each child cuts out the circle. The children then fold the circle in half (a) and then in thirds (b). The circle will then resemble a triangle with one rounded edge. Have each child cut a V-shape from the rounded edge of his or her circle so that the finished snow flake will have six points. Then have the children cut smaller shapes out of the rest of the folded paper (c). After the circle is unfolded, it may be mounted on colored paper and used to decorate a Christmas card or taped on a window to make an effective winter display.

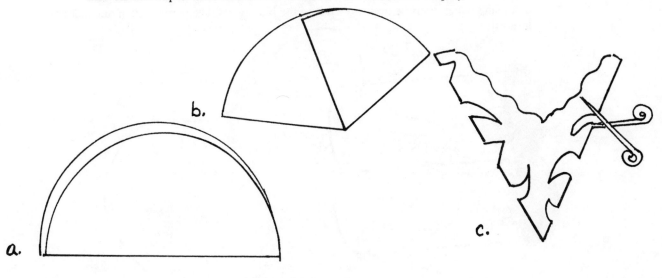

Stringing Necklaces

Materials: Plastic lace, twine or yarn
        Cut up straws
        Variety of objects to string such as Cheerios breakfast cereal, colored construction paper pieces or small styrofoam shapes

Method: Give each child a lace or piece of yarn with a knot tied at one end. The children string objects on the lace or yarn in any order they choose. Tie the two ends of the lace or yarn together when the child finishes stringing to make the necklace.

Printing Tubes

Materials: Empty toilet paper tubes
        Bowls of various colored paints
        Paper
        Colored chalk or crayons (optional)

Method: Place four or five plastic bowls containing different colored paint on the art table. Have the children dip one end of a tube in the paint and then apply it to their papers. When the pictures are dry, the children may color in the circles with chalk or crayon.

Binoculars

Materials: Two empty toilet paper tubes per child
        Cellophane tape
        Paint
        String
        Hole puncher
        Stapler
        Colored cellophane paper

Method: Staple the two tubes together as shown. If the stapler won't fit inside a tube to accomplish this, use tape to secure the tubes together. Have the children paint the binoculars. Punch holes at one end of the binoculars and attach string handles to the holes. Tape colored cellopane paper over the opposite ends of the binoculars. Using more than one color adds interest.

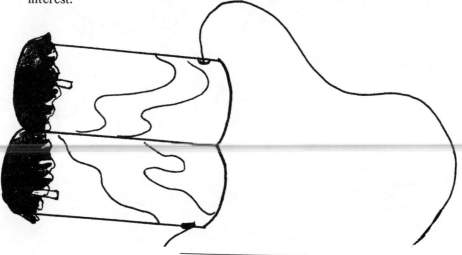

Pom Poms

Materials: Empty toiler paper tubes
12" × 18" tissue paper
Scissors
Paint
Glue

Method: Children paint tubes and allow them to dry. Give each child a sheet of tissue paper folded
lengthwise. Have the child fringe the paper from the cut side to within 1½" to 2" from the
fold.

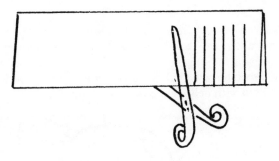

Apply a thin line of glue along the folded edge of the fringed tissue. Place one end of the
tube on one end of the glued portion of the tissue and roll it to the other end so that the
tissue wraps around the tube, sticking to the tube and to itself.

Puzzles

Materials: Large colorful pictures cut from old magazines or calendars
Paste
Felt markers
Scissors
Colored construction paper

Method: Children look through a pile of pictures and select the one they wish to use. Have each child paste his picture on a piece of construction paper. Different colors of construction paper help children identify their own puzzles. When the paste is dry, the children draw lines on their papers with a felt marker to indicate puzzle pieces. If possible, laminate the pictures before cutting. Then the child or teacher cuts along the lines the child has drawn. The children can take turns working each other's puzzles.

Sewing Cards

Materials: Brightly colored pictures of a single object
Hole puncher
Stiff paper such as cardboard, laundry cards, posterboard, etc.
Yarn

Method: Have the children cut out their pictures and paste them on the cardboard or other stiff paper. Leaving about a 1" border, cut the cardboard around the picture so that the hole puncher will reach the edges of the picture. Punch holes about 1½" apart around the picure. Have the children lace their cards with yarn. The ends of the yarn may be stiffened by wrapping them with cellophane tape or dipping them into melted wax.

Leaf People Pictures

Materials: Large leaves
Stapler
Paper
Crayons

Method: On a clear autumn day, take the children on a walk and collect leaves. Staple each leaf to a piece of manila paper. The children draw a head, arms, legs and a background on the paper around the leaf.

Collage

Materials: Scissors
Paste
Construction paper
Variety of items such as wallpaper, cloth remnants, tissue paper, seeds, rice, oatmeal, sand, buttons, cotton balls, string, yarn, macaroni, etc.

Method: Children apply paste to their piece of construction paper and press miscellaneous objects to it to create a collage. If desired, draw or have the children draw an outline of a shape first and fill it in with objects.

Paper Mosaic Pictures

Materials: Stencils of objects such as fish, balloons, stars, etc.
Small pieces of colored construction paper, tissue paper or self-stick paper
Construction paper (whole)

Method: Give each child a piece of construction paper. Have the children trace a stencil on their papers. Then have them paste small pieces of colored paper within the outline.

 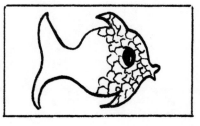

Paper Fans

Materials: Manila or typing paper
Paint
Stapler

Method: The children paint a picture on the paper. When the paper is dry, they fold it fan fashion and staple one end.

Snowfall Pictures

Materials: Typing paper
Black construction paper
Chalk
Hole puncher
Paste

Method: Give each child a piece of dark construction paper and half a sheet of typing paper. Have the child draw a winter scene with chalk on the dark paper. Then he punches "snowflakes" out of the typing paper with the hole puncher and and pastes them on the picture.

Torn Tissue Paper Trees

Materials: Madras tissue paper
              Construction paper
              Glue mixed with water
              Felt marker

Method: Have the children tear the tissue paper into medium sized pieces about 2" × 3". Odd shapes and sizes are ideal. Give each child a piece of construction paper. Either draw or have the children draw tree trunks with felt markers on the construction paper. Then have the children apply glue to the construction paper and stick the pieces of tissue to it. Overlapping causes a "bleeding" effect which will add interest to the picture.

Paper Mache Balloons

Materials: Balloons
              String
              Strips of newspaper
              Liquid laundry starch
              Paint

Methods: Blow up the balloons and tie each one securely. Make sure there is one balloon for each child. Each child dips strips of newspaper into the liquid starch and covers his balloon with them until the paper mache is several layers thick. After the paper mache has dried thoroughly, have the children paint it.

liquid starch

Silhouette Pictures

Materials: A long sheet of brown wrapping paper
            Stencils
            Scissors
            Paste
            Pencils
            Colored construction paper

Method: Children trace stencils on colored construction paper and cut out the figures. The children all paste their figures on the wrapping paper to produce a cooperative mural.

Yarn Pictures

Materials: Construction paper
            Yarn
            Glue or paste
            Colored gravel

Method: Children draw a design with glue or paste on their paper. They apply yarn to the entire glue design or around the edges of the glue design to form an outline. Gravel may be sprinkled on the inside of the design.

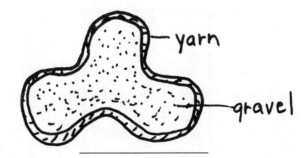

Pasting Inside a Template

Materials: Plastic template
            Paste
            Glitter
            Construction paper

Method: Holding the template steady on a sheet of paper, the child fills in the inside with paste. He then sprinkles glitter on the paste. Remove the template and the child has created a pattern in glitter on the construction paper.

Sand Painting I

Materials: A mixture of one part sand, 1/4 part powdered tempera paint
                Paper
                Paste

Method: Mix the sand and powdered paint together in a shaker. Cover each piece of paper with paste. Shake some of the sand mixture on each paper. Have the child make a design with the sand mixture using his fingers.

Sand Painting II

Materials: Colored sand (see Sand Painting I)
                Glue or paste
                Construction paper

Method: Make colored sand following the directions in Sand Painting I. Have the child draw a design on his paper with glue. The child then sprinkles colored sand all over the paper. When the excess sand is shaken off, the remaining sand adheres to the glue design.

Egg Shell Pictures

Materials: Egg shells broken in half
                Tempera paint
                Paper
                Glue

Method: Wash the egg shells carefully and let them dry. The children then paint them, usually one color on the outside and a different color on the inside. While the paint is drying, children paint pictures on their papers. When the egg shells are dry, the children glue the egg shells on the pictures.

Shoes to Lace

Materials: 5" × 8" posterboard rectangles
                Felt tipped markers
                Yarn
                Scissors
                Hole puncher

Method: Give each child one or two posterboard rectangles, depending on whether they want to trace both of their feet or just one. The child traces a foot on the posterboard rectangle with the marking pen and then cuts it out. With teacher help, he marks eight spots on the shoe and then punches them out. Use yarn as the shoe lace. The ends of the yarn may be dipped into hot wax or wrapped in cellophane to stiffen them. This activity teaches left foot, right foot and encourages the child to learn to tie a bow.

Q-Tip Painting

Materials: Q-tips
Paint
Empty egg cartons
Manila paper

Method: Fill each egg receptacle in the egg carton with a different colored paint and place two or three Q-tips in each one. Children then use the Q-tips as they would a brush to paint their pictures.

Caterpillars

Materials: Cardboard egg cartons cut in half lengthwise
Paint
Pipe cleaners
String

Method: Each child paints an egg carton half to look like a caterpillar, including a face at one end. When the caterpillars are dry, the child inserts pipe cleaners for antennae in the caterpillar's forehead. A string may be attached to the nose for pulling.

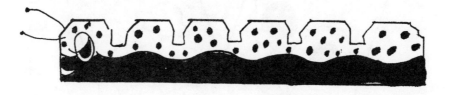

Butterflies

Materials: Butterfly stencils
Paint
Scissors
Paste
Sequins
Straws
Colored construction paper

Method: Each child traces two butterflies from the stencils. After cutting out the butterflies, the child paints them and pastes them together. Insert a straw between the butterflies and secure it in place with staples. Paste on sequins for decoration.

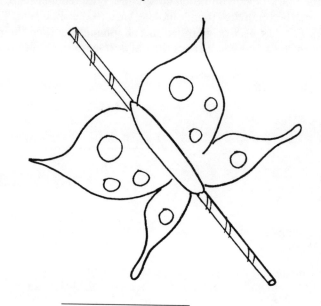

Baking Cup Pictures

Materials: Paper baking cups (either whole or cut in half)
Paste
Paint
Paper

Method: Either have the child paste the baking cups to a piece of paper and draw a picture around it or have the child draw a picture and then paste the cups onto the picture in appropriate places.

Chalkboard Pictures

Materials: White chalk
A chalkboard

Method: The children cover the entire chalkboard with white chalk. Then they take turns drawing pictures on the board with their fingers.

Winter Pictures

NOTE: Chalk pictures may be preserved slightly by spraying them with hair spray.

Materials: Dark colored construction paper
           White chalk

Method: Children draw snow pictures with the white chalk on the dark construction paper.

Wet Chalk Pictures I

Materials: Manila paper
           Colored chalk
           Small bowls of water

Methods: The children dip the end of a piece of chalk into the water and then apply it to the paper.

Wet Chalk Pictures II

Materials: A large dishpan half-filled with water
           Manila paper
           Colored chalk

Method: Each child dips a sheet of paper in the water for a few seconds to wet it all over. Then each child draws a picture on the wet paper with dry chalk.

Wet Chalk Pictures III

Materials: Paper
           Colored chalk
           Paint brushes
           Bowls of water

Method: Children draw pictures with dry chalk, then paint over the chalked parts with a brush and water.

Wet Chalk Pictures IV

Materials: Pans of liquid starch mixed with a little water
           Large paint brushes
           Smooth paper
           Colored chalk

Method: Children paint their papers with starch and then make designs on it with the chalk while the paper is still wet. The starch makes the chalk more permanent.

---

2. Clay

Clay modeling is an activity which assists small muscle development. Substitute materials such as play dough or plastic dough have a definite use, but clay should not be eliminated from any program. Clay is more elastic and "gooier" than the fabricated substances.

With the use of a kiln, clay products attain a "finished" appearance. Even without a kiln, however, the use of clay is still desirable since children enjoy its properties. By painting and shellacking the clay, children can produce attractive items.

Clay is usually kept in a closed stone crock and covered with a damp cloth. It can be purchased in either powdered or moist form and is inexpensive. Approximately one pound per child is suggested for making small objects.

Feel free to explore the possibilities offered by clay in addition to the entertaining activities suggested below:

Clay Snowmen

Materials: Clay
            Toothpicks
            White glaze or paint
            Yarn
            Odds and ends

Method: *With a kiln:* Have the children roll their clay into a large ball. Have them indent the upper third of the ball to form a head. After it is thoroughly dry, fire the clay. Glaze the snowman and fire it again. Put yarn around the snowman's neck for a scarf and glue on the other decorations.

Without a kiln: Have the children roll their clay into two balls: a large ball for the body and a smaller one for the head. Insert a toothpick into the top of the body and stick the head on it. If necessary, use glue to make the head more secure on the body. The clay must then dry thoroughly for several days, preferably in the sun. Have the children paint the snowman. Then let it dry again and shellack it. Yarn and other decorations add the finishing touches.

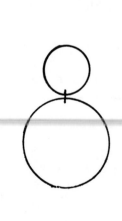

Pencil or Candle Holders

Materials: Clay
First grade pencils
Paint or glaze

Method: Allow the chiuldren to make their own basic form out of the clay. Have them insert the unsharpened end of a pencil into the clay to make depressions. When it is thoroughly dried, fire the pencil holder, or else let the children paint and shellack it.

3. Stencils and Patterns

Stencils may be used freely as well as purposefully. They can be traced or sponged around, colored, painted, pasted in, cut out, collaged, "glittered," or stapled together and stuffed.

The teacher should construct the patterns from heavy material such as cardboard or posterboard. (Montessori classrooms usually have shape templates or designs with metal insets for children to trace.)

Butterfly

Place the body of the butterfly pattern on the fold of a sheet of colored construction paper folded in half. Trace the butterfly with a pencil and then cut it out. Make sure whoever does the cutting does not cut on the fold. The child may staple colored cellophane or tissue paper to the opening in the wings. These butterflies make an effective window display.

Yellow Jacket

Place the straight side of the yellow jacket pattern on the fold of a sheet of yellow construction paper folded in half. After the child traces and cuts out the yellow jacket—making sure not to cut along the fold—he may decorate it with black paint.

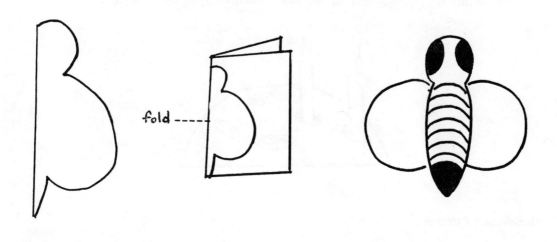

Frog

Each child traces and cuts out one body and four feet. Then give the child eight strips of paper to fold for the four legs. (See *Circle Puppets on a String* at page 37 for directions for making the legs.) Attach the feet to the bottom of each leg and staple each leg to the frog's body.

Birds

Have the children trace simple semi-circles, cut them out and decorate them to make bird caricatures.

Fish

Make fish by using two basic geometric shapes or using a more elaborate pattern.

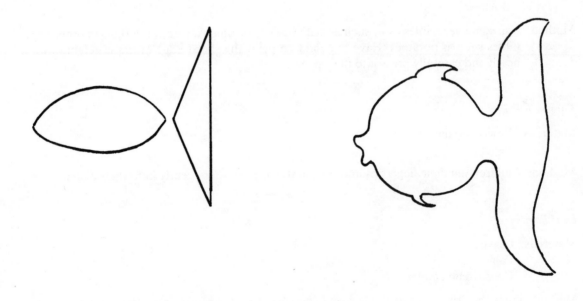

---

4. Printmaking

Fruit Prints (Apples, Oranges, Lemons, Grapefruit, etc.)

Materials: Fruit cut in half
           Thick tempera paint
           Construction paper

Method: Dip the cut side of a fruit into paint. Wipe off the excess paint on the edge of the bowl. Then press the fruit onto a piece of construction paper.

APPLES

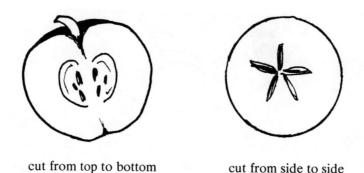

cut from top to bottom   cut from side to side

Vegetable Prints (Carrots, Potatoes, Beets, Radishes, etc.)

Materials: Fresh crisp vegetables (sliced)
         Paint
         Paper
         Brushes

Method: Use some vegetables as is, such as sliced celery or onions. Cut out designs in other vegetables such as potatoes. Have the children paint the sliced edge of the vegetable with a brush and carefully press it to their papers.

Fingertip Prints

Materials: Bowls of paint
         Paper

Method: Children dip their fingertips into the paint and press them gently onto their papers.

Leaf Prints

Materials: Leaves
         Paint
         Construction paper

Method: Paint the "rib" sides of the leaves. (The rib sides are used because they make a sharper print.) Children place their painted leaf on a clean piece of newspaper. Then they press a sheet of manila paper on the leaf. A brayer may be used to roll over the paper. The leaf leaves its imprint on the manila paper. Laminated, these leaf prints make effective gifts.

---

5. Paper Plate Crafts

The possible uses of paper plates are limitless. They can be turned into faces, clocks, masks, telephone dials, suns, moons, fancy frisbees, flowers, lollipops, and more. You can cut them up, cut them out, string them up, fringe them or staple them.

Only a few ideas have been included here to demonstrate the use of paper plates. They should inspire you to think of many more.

Tambourines

Materials: Two paper plates per child
     Bottle caps
     Paint
     Yarn
     Hole puncher
     Stapler

Method: Each child paints the backs of two paper plates. When the plates are dry, insert several bottle caps between each pair of plates and staple them together around the edges. Punch holes around the edge of each tambourine and tie yarn through each hole for decoration.

Pot Holder Holders

Materials: 1½ paper plates per child
     Paint
     Shellac
     Stapler

Method: Have the children decorate the plate and the plate half. Staple the plate half to the whole plate to form a pocket. The holders may be shellacked. If children use looms, they may put the pot holders they make in the pocket and take the holders home on Mother's Day.

Hand Prints on Paper Plates

Materials: Paper plates
     Paint
     Brushes

Method: Children paint one of their hands with thick tempera paint and then press it to the center of a paper plate. They may decorate the edges of the plate if they wish.

33

Sunshine Faces

Materials: Paper plates
           Scissors
           Yellow cellophane
           Stapler

Method: Children cut out the inner portion of a paper plate and staple yellow cellophane across the hole in the plate. They enjoy looking through these plates during the day.

———————————

Stitching Plates

Materials: Paper plates
           Yarn
           Plastic embroidery needles
           Hole puncher

Method: The children or teacher punches holes around the edge of a paper plate. Using a needle or yarn that has had its end dipped into wax, the children stitch the plate with yarn as they please.

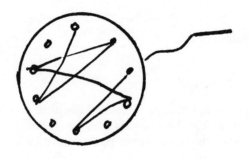

———————————

Paper Plate Collage With Tissue Paper

Materials: Liquid starch
           Paper plates
           Strips of various colored tissue paper or crepe paper

Method: Paint the backs of the paper plates with liquid starch. Use the painted plate as a background for applying strips of colored tissue or crepe paper in overlapping designs. The colors may "bleed" through but the bleeding makes the design more effective.

———————————

Chinese Hats

These can be made for Chinese New Year.

Materials: Paper plates
           Scissors
           Hole puncher
           Paint
           Yarn

Method: Children decorate their plates with paint. The teacher then cuts a slit half way through it. Lap one cut edge over the other slightly to form a cone and staple. Punch holes on opposite sides near the edge of the plate and insert yarn to serve as a tie to hold the hat in place on the child's heat.

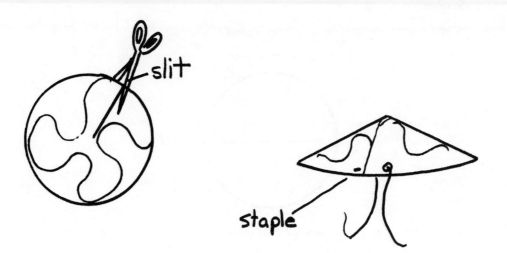

Turtles

Materials: Paper plates
Green construction paper
Paint
Black felt-tipped marker
Stapler

Method: Children paint the plate green. When the plate is dry, they draw black lines on it to make the plate look like the back of a turtle. Children then staple legs and a head cut out of construction paper to the turtle's body and decorate the turtle as they wish.

Hand Puppet

Materials: Two paper plates for each child
              Egg carton
              Paint
              Shredded "Easter grass"
              Stapler

Method: Slit one paper plate across the center almost to the edges.

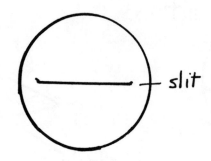

Staple two egg carton sections for eyes on one side of the slit.

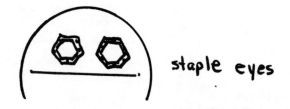

Place the slit paper plate over another plate and staple all around the edges. Decorate the plates. Make sure the inside of the puppet's mouth gets decorated also. Fold both plates along the slit. Slip hand inside the slit to manipulate the puppet.

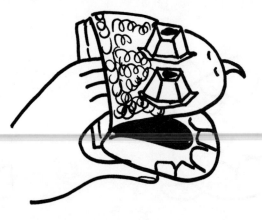

6. Puppets

Puppets may be constructed out of socks, paper bags, paper plates, paper mache on light bulbs, paper towel tubes, etc. The following three examples are simple and inexpensive.

Circle Puppets on a String

Materials: Construction paper circles in two sizes: one for the head and a larger one for the body
Eight strips of paper per puppet
Paint
Buttons
Felt markers
Stapler
Hole puncher

Method: Children cut out two construction paper circles and decorate them. Then they staple the circles together and make the puppet's arms and legs. Each arm and leg requires two strips of paper. The two strips are stapled at right angles to each other onto the body. The bottom strip is folded back over the top strip beginning close to the puppet's body (1). The second strip now becomes the bottom strip and it is folded back over the top strip (2). This folding action is repeated until the child has reached the end of the paper strips. A zig-zag pattern will result. Staple the end of the arm or leg to hold it. Punch a hole at the top of the puppet's head and insert a loop of string.

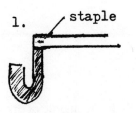

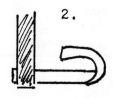

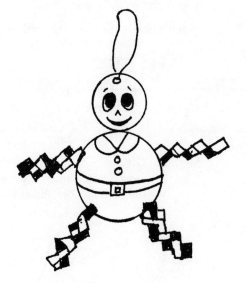

Stick Puppets

Materials: Wooden tongue depressors
Glue
Plastic lids from yogurt or other containers
Circles of cloth, 8" in diameter
Buttons
Felt
Marking pens
Yarn

37

Method: Cut a slit in the center of the cloth circle and slip it over the tongue depressor. Glue it down. This is the puppet's dress. Glue a circle of construction paper to the inside of the plastic lid. Staple the lid to the tongue depressor. Decorate the construction paper face with yarn for hair, buttons for eyes, felt for a mouth, etc.

Styrofoam Ball Puppets

Materials: Oval styrofoam balls
　　　　　Circles of cloth 8" or 9" in diameter
　　　　　Yarn
　　　　　Felt
　　　　　Marking pens
　　　　　Scrap material
　　　　　Sharpened pencils
　　　　　Cellophane tape

Method: Give each child a styrofoam ball to decorate for a face. Cut a small slit in the middle of the cloth circle. Insert a pencil through the slit. Use cellophane tape to secure the cloth to the pencil. Then insert the point of the pencil into the bottom of the styrofoam head.

By turning the table on its side, you can create a puppet "stage." One or two children, operating the puppets, may sit behind it and put on a show.

7. Flowers

Tissue Paper Flowers I

Materials: Madras tissue paper
Scissors
Straws
Stapler

Method: Either the teacher or the child cuts out circles, 3" or 4" in diameter, from the tissue paper. The children then fringe the edges of the circles, usually cutting through three or four circles at a time. The teacher then staples the circles to the end of a straw.

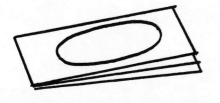

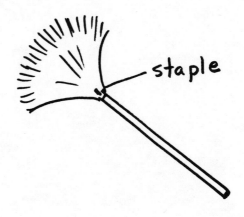

Tissue Paper Flowers II

Materials: Tissue paper petals
Glue
Pipe cleaners

Method: Give the children tissue paper petals. They glue one petal at a time around a pipe cleaner beginning at the top and working their way down. Staple the petals to the pipe cleaner to reinforce them.

Tissue Paper Flowers III

Materials: Strips of tissue paper
Pipe cleaners
Gummed tape
Stapler

Method: Fold the strips of tissue paper lengthwise. Wrap the strip around a finger. Pinch the bottom shut and staple it to hold. Insert a pipe cleaner as a stem and tape it to hold.

B. HOLIDAY ART

1. Halloween

Paper Bag or Pillow Case Costumes

Materials: Large paper bags from the grocery store or old pillow cases
           Paint
           Felt markers
           Scissors
           Felt
           Yarn
           Glue

Method: If using paper bags, the teacher cuts out a face hole and arm holes. If using pillow cases, the teacher cuts out eye holes. Children decorate the costumes with materials available.

Paper Plate Masks

Materials: Paper plates
           Yarn
           Paint
           Hole puncher
           Scissors

Method: The teacher cuts out eye holes and the children decorate the plates as masks. Punch holes in and attach strings to each side of the plate to hold the mask on the child's head.

Trick or Treat Bags

Materials: Medium sized paper bags from the grocery store
            Yarn
            Paint
            Scissors
            Cardboard

Method: Staple yarn to the top of the bags to form a handle. Children decorate the bags with available materials. Cut the cardboard to fit the bottom of the bag and put it in to reinforce the bottom of the bag.

Pine Cone Owls

Materials: 4" cardboard circles
            4" green felt circles
            Pine cones
            Glue
            White or yellow felt eyes
            Brown felt ears
            Red felt mouths
            Black paint

Method: Glue the green felt circles to the cardboard circles. Glue a pine cone to the center of the green circle. If the pine cones need painting, they may be painted brown. Glue eyes, ears, and mouths on the pine cone and trim them with black paint.

---

2. United Nations Day

Materials: 8½" × 12' white construction paper
Strips of various colored paper
Stars
Bars
Circles
Moons
Scissors
Glue

Method: Give each child a sheet of white paper. He or she constructs his own flag using the materials provided. To carry this project further, children can name their own country and describe its most important laws. For instance, does the country have a president or a king?

_____

3. Thanksgiving

Pine Cone Turkeys

Materials: Pine cones
Manila paper tails
Red construction paper heads
Paint
Glue

Method: Children paint the pine cones and set them aside to dry. They decorate the tails and insert each one into a cone. Then they stick the turkey's head into the small end of the cone. A drop of glue will help hold the head in place.

_____

Hand Turkeys

Materials: Manila paper
         Crayons
         Paint
         Felt markers

Method: Children each trace one hand on a piece of paper and then color it to resemble a turkey. With teacher assistance, the children add feet and eyes.

Alternative Method: Each child paints one of his hands (brown palm, colorful fingers) and prints it on a piece of paper. The children draw in feet and eyes with felt markers.

Apple Turkeys

These turkeys can also be made with oranges, potatoes, and other suitable fruits and vegetables.

Materials: Apples (or other fruit or vegetable)
         Tail and head cutouts or stencils
         Paint
         Toothpicks

Method: Children trace, cut out and paint tails and heads. When the tails are dry, the children insert them in a slit in the apple. They then insert the head and place toothpicks on the bottom for feet and to balance the turkey.

4. Christmas

Funny Santas

Materials: Outlines of Santas on white construction paper drawn by the teacher
         Paint
         Cotton balls
         Glitter
         Ribbon

Method: Children finish the picture with materials furnished by the teacher.

teacher's drawing

Christmas Tree Ornament

Materials: Empty toilet paper tubes
Paint
Cotton
Glitter
Red yarn
Hole puncher

Method: Children decorate the tubes with paint, cotton, glitter, etc. When the tubes are finished, the children punch two holes near the top of each tube and insert the yarn to mak a handle.

Paper Plate Angels

Materials: Paper plates
Small poster board circles
Paint
Glue
Tissue paper

Method: The teacher assists the children as they cut off "wings" from the paper plates. The wings are fastened to the body with brads or staples. The children draw a face on the small posterboard circle and then staple it to the body. Using watered glue, the children paste torn strips of colored tissue on the body. Pale blue tissue is most effective.

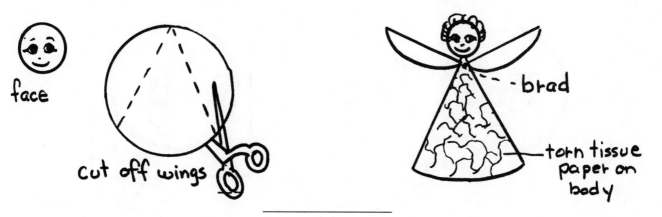

45

Santa Cookie Tins

Materials: Empty coffee tins or oatmeal boxes
              Paint
              Cotton
              Red paper circles

Method: The children decorate the boxes to resemble Santa. Each red circle is stapled to form a cone hat and placed on a Santa.

NOTE: Children may bake cookies and fill the containers as a gift.

Christmas Cards

Materials: Christmas cookie cutters
              Heavy red and white yarn
              9" green construction paper circles
              Glue
              Pencils

Method: Children trace cookie cutter designs on the green circles. They glue yarn to the outline of the design and then fill in the design with yarn. Then the children cover the outline of the circle with yarn. These circles are then glued on a folded piece of construction paper to make a card.

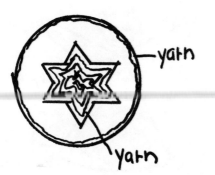

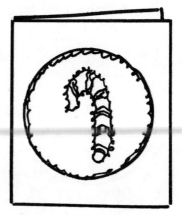

Ice Cream Cone Christmas Trees

Materials: Cones for ice cream
           Gold spray paint
           Sequins
           Glitter
           Colored life savers
           Glue

Method: Spray the cones gold. When the cones are dry, glue sequins, glitter or candy on them for decoration.

Paper Plate Wreath

Materials: Paper plates
           Ribbon
           Tissue paper
           Glitter
           Scissors
           Stapler

Method: If they are capable, have the children cut out the center of their plates. They glue small crumpled squares of green tissue paper on the paper plate rings. If they desire, they may sprinkle the tissue paper with glitter. The teacher staples a red bow to the top of each wreath.

Mexican Candle Holders to Decorate the Christmas Table

Materials: Various sized tin cans
           Terry cloth towel
           Hammer and nails
           A stubby or votive candle

Method: Remove outer wrapping from cans that have been opened completely at one end. Wash and fill each with water. Place in a freezer until frozen solid. Fold the towel. Lay each can sideways on the towel and, using the hammer and nails, punch holes in the can in a design. Melt the ice. Place a candle in the center of each holder. It is best to place a small dish under each candle. Add greenery around the base of the candle for decoration.

folded towel

5. New Year

New Year's Calendar

Materials: 12" × 18" colored posterboard for each child
Stencil for a frame with an inside measurement of 8½" × 12"
Small calendar
Paint
Paper

Method: Have the children trace the frame stencil on their posterboard and decorate the frame they've drawn. They then glue the calendar above or underneath the frame. Children paint a winter picture which they tape inside the frame. Each month, the child paints a new picture to be placed in the frame.

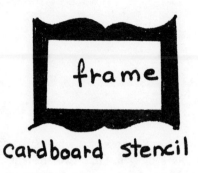

frame

cardboard stencil

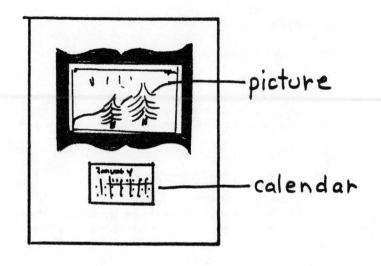

picture

calendar

6. Rosh Hashana (Jewish New Year)

Materials: Emtpy toilet tissue tubes
             Ram's horn stencils
             Paint
             Stapler

Method: Children stencil two Ram's horns each, cut them out and decorate them with paint. They then staple the horns on either side of the empty tube. The children pretend to blow them as they would horns.

ram's horn pattern

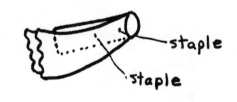

staple

staple

7. Hanukkah

Hanukkah Handprints

Materials: White construction paper
             Paint
             Colored construction paper

Method: Children paint one hand with tempera paint and print it on white construction paper. They may use many colors and make many handprints. Mounted on colored construction paper and then laminated, the handprint makes an impressive Hanukkah gift. If desired, the children can prepare a short poem such as the one which follows to accompany the handprint.

        Everyday I'm growing and soon I'll be quite tall
        So here's a little handprint to remind you of when I
           was small

8. Birthdays

George Washington (Revolutionary Soldiers)

Materials: Empty toilet tissue tubes
                Blue paint
                Strips of white and blue construction paper
                Curved strips of black construction paper
                Paste
                Marking pen

Method: Paint the bottom half of a tube blue. When the tube is dry, criss cross two white strips across the front and draw a face above the strips with a marking pen. Glue two straight blue strips on each side for arms. Staple the three curved black strips together to form a three-pointed hat to fit on the tube. The hat should be approximately 2½" from outer edge to outer edge.

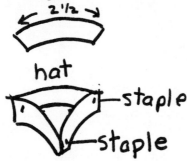

Abraham Lincoln's Cabin

Materials: 12" × 18" manila paper
                Scissors
                Corrugated paper
                Red construction paper
                Paint
                Paste

Method: Give children pieces of corrugated paper, cut to 5" × 7", for cabins. They cut out a door and window in the corrugated paper and paste it on the manila paper. They paste a red construction paper roof over the cabin and paint a scene around the cabin.

Martin Luther King Crowns

Materials: Construction paper
               String
               Hole puncher
               Marking pen

Method: Draw a crown on the construction paper. Have the children cut out crowns and copy the name: "Martin Luther." Punch holes on each end of the crown and insert strings through each hole.

9. Valentine's Day

Valentine Boxes

Materials: Empty tissue boxes
               Paint
               Paste
               Paper doilies
               Various sized red or white paper hearts cut out of construction paper

Method: Children paint the boxes red, allow them to dry and decorate them with materials provided by the teacher.

Valentines

Materials: Heart stencils
               White and red construction paper
               Scissors
               Paste
               Glitter
               Paper doilies

Method: Let the children experiment and create original Valentines from the materials you have provided them.

Hearts

Materials: Large cardboard heart stencils
               Small squares of colored tissue paper
               Paste
               Red construction paper
               Pencils
               Scissors

Method: Children trace hearts on red construction paper and cut them out. They wad up small squares of colored tissue paper, one at a time, and paste them in patterns on the heart.

Valentine Mail Box

An activity to complement Valentine crafts is to have the children build a post office with large blocks and prepare a large envelope for each child. The children mail their Valentines and the postmaster (teacher) sorts them into the proper envelopes. Two or three children become mailmen and distribute the mail at the end of the day.

10. Easter

Easter Bonnets

Materials: Paper plates
Paint
Ribbon
Ruffled crepe paper
Hole puncher

Method: The children decorate the paper plates with paint. When the paint is dry, the children staple ruffled crepe paper around the the edges of the plate. Punch holes on either side of the plate and insert ribbon ties.

Easter Egg Tree

Materials: Construction paper
                Egg patterns
                Various colored strips of paper
                Felt markers

Method: Cover a bulletin board with light colored construction paper. In the center, draw a tree. Children trace and cut out eggs. They decorate them with colored strips by pasting and trimming. They then tack the eggs on the tree.

If you wish, add or have the children add as a community project grass, flowers and bunnies to the bulletin board scene.

---

11. May Day

May Baskets

Materials: Plastic berry baskets
                Green paper squares cut to fit the bottom of the baskets or Easter grass
                Colored yarn
                Tissue paper flowers

Method: Dip the ends of the yarn in hot wax or wrap them in cellophane tape to make them stiff for weaving. Then have the children weave the yarn through the berry baskets. Place green paper or Easter grass in the bottom of the baskets. Have the children make paper flowers (see *Flowers* at page 39) and fill their baskets with them.

May Flowers Headband

Materials: Pipe cleaners
                Masking tape
                Cellophane tape
                Crepe paper
                Paper flowers

Method: The teacher twists the ends of two pipe cleaners together to form a circle. Reinforce the pipe cleaners with masking tape at the connections. Then twist crepe paper around the circle and secure it in place with cellophane tape. Have the children make tissue paper or crepe paper flowers (see *Flowers* at page 39) and glue them to the headband. The teacher may want to reinforce the glue by stapling the flowers in place.

12. Mother's Day

Silhouettes

Materials: Black paper
White paper
High intensity lamp

Method: Each child is placed between the light and a black sheet of paper so that his silhouette is focused on the paper. The teacher traces the silhouette and cuts it out. Children then paste their own silhouettes on a sheet of white paper. The silhouettes may be gift wrapped and sent home for Mother's Day.

Corsages

Materials: Tissue paper flowers
Pipe cleaners
Paper doilies
Glue
Glitter
Clear plastic wrap

Method: Each child makes several tissue paper flowers. (See *Flowers* at page 39). Then each child paints the edge of a paper doily with glue and dips it into gold glitter. The teacher wraps a doily around the flowers and secures it by stapling. Cover the corsages with plastic to protect them until it is time for the children to take them home to Mother.

Recipe Books

Materials: Paper
A duplicating machine
Colore construction paper
Markers

Method: Have each child bring a recipe from home. Arrange the recipes in order, duplicate them and compile them into booklets. List each child's name below the recipe he or she donated. Make covers for the booklets out of construction paper. Let the children decorate their own recipe books as they please and give them to their mothers.

---

13. Father's Day

Bookmark I

Materials: Strips of colored posterboard 1½" × 4"
Glue
Clear contact paper
Small sized school photograph of each child
Ribbon

Method: Glue the child's picture to one end of the posterboard strip. Glue the end of a ribbon above the picture. If desired, decorate the bookmark with felt markers. Cover the entire bookmark with clear contact paper for durability.

Bookmark II

Materials: Burlap strips
Felt shapes
Glue
Yarn (optional)

Method: The children paste felt shapes on the burlap strips and, if necessary, the teacher trims the edges for them. Yarn may be tied at the bottom of the bookmark as trim, if desired.

Paper Weights

Materials: Large stones
Paint
Shellac

Method: Take the children on a walk and have them collect large stones. After the rocks are washed and allowed to dry, the children paint and then shellac them.

The ultimate goals of an early childhood program in language arts are to imbue the child with the desire to learn to read and to plant the seeds for an appreciation of literature.

If teachers provide a diversified program, children will progress at their own speed in their own way. It is desirable to schedule informal lessons in the curriculum. They may involve the entire class, a small group, or in some instances, individual children.

Using the eclectic approach, and borrowing techniques from various systems, we present the following areas for teachers of young children:
A. Listening
B. Speaking
C. Pre-reading
D. Pre-writing
E. Spelling
F. Poetry

A. LISTENING

Listening skills can be taught. When acquired in the very early years, listening skills become habits that prepare the child for future scholastic demands. Ideally, constant exposure to proper language structure will make a positive impression on the child. Through short daily lessons such as the ones listed below, children can be given the opportunity to listen, assimilate and internalize.

Words Spoken in Context

During conversation time, the teacher makes up statements and omits the last word so the child has the opportunity to supply an answer. Any reasonable statement on the part of the child is acceptable. Example: "We went to the drugstore and bought some _____."

Riddle Game

This exercise is used to help children identify letter sounds. The teacher describes an object, "It spins and is a toy and begins with a _____." (sounding the "t" as it is used in the word). A second example: "It has four legs and barks and begins with a _____." (sounding the "d" as it is used in the word). The children guess the answers to the riddles.

What I Saw

One child is "it" and says, "On my way to school today, I saw a _____." Then the child imitates what he or she saw. Children take turns guessing what the answer is. The student who guesses the right answer has the next turn as "it."

Name the Story

The teacher reads a short story to the children and then asks them to suggest a name for it.

Listening for Beginning Sounds

Since vowels have more than one sound, it is recommended that you give beginners initial consonant sounds to identify. Display several familiar objects on a table. (For example, a hat, a book, soap, a feather, etc.) The teacher then asks, "Can someone give me something that begins with a (initial consonant) sound?" Use the sound of the letter instead of the letter name. Encourage the children to volunteer to come up and select the proper object.

Alphabet Boxes

Use a shoebox as the Alphabet Box. Stand the lid of the box upright against the box and use it to display the letter of the week. Select a different letter each week and tape it to the inside of the box lid. After you have taped up the letter of the week, draw it to the children's attention and have the children listen to the sound of the letter. Give them examples of words which begin with the sound. Ask the children to give examples also. During the week, ask the children to bring in objects or pictures of things which begin with the letter and place them in the box. At the end of the week, go through the contents of the box with the children, naming each item and emphasizing the letter's sound.

Identifying Objects with Like Initial Sounds

The teacher holds up three pictures for a group of children to observe. Two show items which have like initial sounds (for example, a ball and a bat). The third shows an item with a different initial sound (for example, candy). The children must identify the two items which have like sounds.

Matching Initial Sounds

The teacher prints the capital and lower case forms of one letter on the chalkboard. She then pronounces two or three words that begin with the same sound. For example, after writing "M, m" she might say "monkey" and "man." She then asks the children to contribute other words which begin with the same sound. As the children say different words, the teacher prints them on the board and draws simple pictures of what they represent.

Rhyming

The teacher begins the lesson by rhyming two words (for example, "floor" and "door"). She then asks the children to think of other words that rhyme with the words she has given.

Rhyming Word Worms

Cut out a large number of small paper circles. Draw a face on enough of the circles so that each child can have one. Choose a basic word and print it on enough circles so that each child can also have one of these. Leave the rest of the circles blank. Give each child a worm's face, several blank circles and one circle containing the printed word. Have the children fill in the blank circles with words that rhyme with the given word. Staple the circles together. The more rhyming words, the longer the worm.

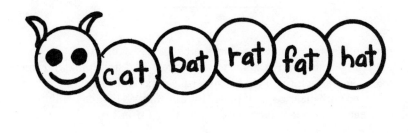

Initial Consonant Board

Draw eighteen squares on a large sheet of posterboard and print consonants in the upper righthand corner of each square. Omit C, Q and X since they have no sounds of their own. Prepare small cards by drawing or pasting on each one a picture of an object. Have the child pick up a card, sound out the name of the object, and place it on its matching initial consonant square. For example, the child will place a picture of a sun on the "S" square.

Rhyming Board

Paste nine or more pictures of objects on a large piece of brightly colored posterboard. Prepare picture cards of objects which rhyme with the objects pasted to the board. The child places the picture cards on the rhyming object pictured on the posterboard.

Alliteration Game

The teacher picks a letter. Then she asks the children to say or write sentences in which all the words begin with that letter. (Use of small words such as "a," "an," and "the" is permitted.) For example:

       "Mother made me mad."
       "Peter painted a picture."
       "She sang a sad song."
       "Cathy crumbled her cookies."

Phonics Flip Cards

Prepare basic cards containing key phrase endings such as "ay," "ot," "on," "it," "at," "id," "un," etc. Attach each basic card to a snap ring similar to those found on notebooks. Prepare smaller cards containing consonants and attach them to the snap ring also. The cards may be constructed out of posterboard and covered with clear contact paper for durability. Have the children form the various words by combining each consonant card with the basic card in turn. Have the children read the words they form to partners or to you.

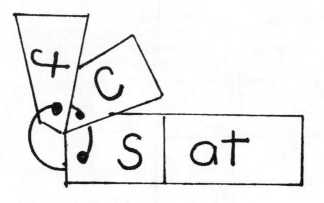

Bingo

Cut cards, 5" × 7", out of posterboard and divide each one into six sections. Make enough cards so that each child in the class will have one. Cut up small squares of construction paper to use to cover the sections during play. Fill in the sections of the bingo cards with capital letters, small letters, numerals, words, etc. Then play bingo. Several methods of playing are:
   1. One at a time, the teacher writes a letter (or numeral or word) on the chalkboard and calls its name;
   2. The teacher writes the letter, numeral or word on the chalkboard but does not call its name;
   3. The teacher calls the letter, numeral or word but does not write it on the chalkboard.

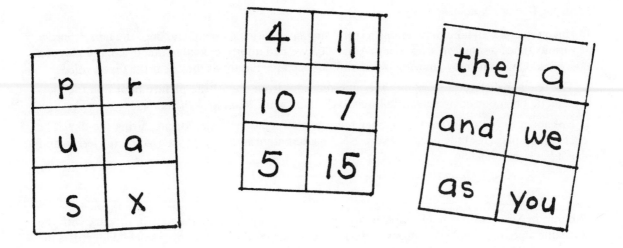

Name Bingo

Give each child a card with his or her name printed on it in large bold letters. Make cards with just first names for younger children. Using a deck of large alphabet letters, one child or the teacher holds up a letter and calls out its name. Children with name bingo cards containing the letter cover it with a chip or small rectangle of construction paper. The first child to cover all the letters on his or her card wins and can be the next caller.

Ideas for Use of Audio Machines

1. Have the children take turns telling a story, singing, reciting a poem, etc., into the tape recorder at various times during the school day. After all have had a turn, assemble the group and play the tape back. Children enjoy guessing the identity of each performer as they hear the taped voices.

2. The teacher dictates a story into the tape recorder from one of the picture books on the class bookshelf. Then one or two children listen to the tape while looking at the book.

3. Unknown to the children, the teacher records conversations which occur during the day. The teacher then plays the tape back as a surprise. An alternative activity is to tape a directed lesson and play it back immediately.

———————————

Lesson in Phonics

Children in Montessori schools, after many exercises in phonics, may then begin to work with the moveable alphabet (wooden or plastic letters). Using a series of picture cards, the child identifies the picture, sounds out the name phonetically and builds words with the letters to match the sounds.

———————————

B. SPEAKING

Spoken language is our first means of communication. The pronounciation of words and voice intonations are basic characteristics of all languages. These two aspects plus an adequate vocabulary enable us to express our thoughts.

Teachers need to set an example when speaking. Use complete sentences whenever possible, particularly during group conversations. In addition, a child's oral language development will be encouraged through his or her use of equipment that stimulates dramatic play situations, such as play telephones, playhouse furniture, costumes, dolls, toy animals, blocks, etc. Also, the same audio machines that promote auditory discrimination are equally valuable to oral development. Finally, by establishing an atmosphere that invites spontaneous expressions, the teacher will help the child gain the self-confidence necessary for oral communication.

Assignment of Jobs

The teacher may assign to children a variety of jobs during the day, such as passing out napkins, calling the roll, turning off lights, holding doors, etc. These shared responsibilities will enhance children's language development.

Dictating a Group Letter

Many occasions call for group letters. The children may wish to thank a parent for a gift to the class, express their appreciation for a successful field trip, send a farewell note to a student moving out of town, etc. First, have the children discuss the purpose of the letter, the sentiments they wish to express to the recipient, the information they wish to convey in the letter, etc. Then let the children take turns dictating sentences. Print the letter as it is dictated by the children on a chart tablet in front of the entire group using a black felt tipped marker so the children can easily observe the letter taking shape. When the letter is complete, let all the children sign their names on it.

Descriptive Stories

Display action pictures to the children and encourage them to describe what they see. Then give each child the opportunity to select a colorful picture. Let the child paste it on a 12" × 18" piece of manila paper and dictate a short story about the picture to the teacher. Print the child's story under the picture as he tells it. Read all the stories to the class or tack them on the bulletin board.

"Reading" Picture Books

Working with a small group, the teacher "reads" a picture book that contains no words. A variety of these picture books are available at book stores. Give a child the opportunity to "read" the same book or a different one to the group.

Cumulative Stories

Children sit in a circle. The teacher initiates a story with a topic that interests the children. (For example, "Once upon a time there was a lazy bear," or "Once upon a time there was a tiny, tiny man.") Going around the circle, each child adds a line to the story.

Rhythmic Clapping

Teach the children the following pattern: Clap, clap, pause. Clap, clap, pause. With each clap say a word and indicate that the child is to fill in the pause with a word. For example:

Clap, clap, pause
"I like _____" (child supplies word)

Spend enough time establishing the rhythm so the exercise becomes an easy game for the children.

Linguistic Exercises

Explain that some words have more than one meaning. Suggest a multiple meaning word such as train, pet, sock, miss, or like. Then give the children examples of the word's different meanings. (For example, "I like to ride on a *train.*" "Did you *train* your dog to sit up?") After the children become familiar with the procedure, name other words and have the children volunteer examples of uses of their various meanings.

Poems for Choral Reading

Although verse choirs may be too difficult for young children, there are many poems with repetitive characteristics which lend themselves to group readings. Three examples follow, which range from the simplest form to more complicated material that is suitable for primary grades.

The Train

The tran goes hurrying over the track	(teacher)
Clickety, clickety, clickety!	(all)
It goes away but it always comes back.	(teacher)
Clickety, clickety, clickety!	(all)
The engineer leans from his window up high.	(teacher)
Clickety, clickety, clickety!	(all)
He waves to me as the train goes by.	(teacher)
Clickety, clickety, clickety!	(all)
I'd like to go, but I want to come back.	(teacher)
Clickety, clickety, clickety!	(all)

Unknown

Coaster Wagon

Down the hill in our wagon we go,	(teacher)
Bumpity, bump, bump, bump—	(girls)
Over the stones with squeaks and groans	(teacher)
And jolts that reach to the ends of our bones,	
Down the hill in our wagon we go—	
Bumpity, bump, bump, BUMP.	(boys)
Our wagon is not a streamlined one,	(teacher)
Bumpity, bump, bump, bump—	(girls)
It's stiff in the joints, but it still can run,	(teacher)
And we go pretty fast when we've once begun;	
Our wagon is old, but it's lot of fun—	
Bumpity, bump, bump, BUMP.	(boys)

Unknown

The Goblin

A goblin lives in our house, in our house, in our house,	High voices
A goblin lives in our house all the year round.	
He bumps and he jumps and he thumps and he stumps.	Low voices
He knocks and he rocks and he rattles at the locks.	Medium voices
A goblin lives in our house, in our house, in our house,	High voices
A goblin lives in our house all the year round.	All

Unknown

C. PRE-READING

Contacts with informal, functional reading should be an integral part of the early learning environment. Name cards on coat hooks, objects in the room that are labelled, an alphabet that is displayed, manuscript memoranda on the chalkboard, labels on bulletin boards, a typewriter and a standing chart tablet are all contributing mechanisms.

The young student who is constantly exposed to letters, numerals and words will feel at home with them in future scholastic situations. The following activities contribute to making a dynamic program.

Color Identification

Give each child a different colored balloon to blow up and hang on the bulletin board. The child may paint the first letter of its color on the balloon. (For example, he will paint a "B" on a blue balloon.)

_____

Color Booklets

The teacher prepares color booklets to be used by the individual children. Label each page with the name of a color. If you wish, write it in the subject color for easy identification. Children either draw pictures using only that color on the page or cut out pictures from magazines of objects in that color and paste them on the page.

_____

Recognition of Fundamental Shapes

Ask children to identify objects in the room and describe their shape. Examples are: clock—circle; flag—rectangle. Have the children identify both two and three dimensional figures.

_____

Matching Pictures with Silhouettes

The teacher prepares two sets of cards, one with pictures of objects and the other with their identical silhouettes. Have the children match them.

_____

Matching Shapes

The teacher cuts out pairs of shapes from colored construction paper, such as two blue triangles, two red squares, etc. Hide one set of the shapes around the room and put the other set in a basket on the teacher's desk. Have the children search the room for shapes. When a child finds a hidden shape, he is to match it with its identical shape in the basket and identify the shape. The child may then keep the two shapes.

_____

Flash Cards of Shapes

Make a series of flash cards, each of which contains pictures of several shapes. If you wish, make the cards progressively more difficult. You may also use commercially manufactured cards, if available. Flash one of the cards in front of a group of children. Remove the card and have the children try to remember all the shapes on it.

Matching Letters

The teacher writes or prints three or four rows of letters on the chalkboard. Put two identical letters in each row. Children take turns circling the pairs. Example:

```
c  l  y  x  s  y  t  u  m  i  o
a  k  u  s  a  y  z  n  e  w  t
b  l  p  g  t  h  m  k  b  s  z
```

Alphabet Matching Exercise

Prepare two sets of identical alphabet cards. Pass one set out to the children. Hold up the cards from the other set one at a time. The child with the displayed card's duplicate brings it to the teacher and identifies the letter.

Arranging the Alphabet in Order

Provide the children with a box of alphabet letters. Include both upper and lower case letters. Children take turns arranging the letters in alphabetical order.

Folded Pictures

Children search through magazines for full page pictures, cut them out, and fold them accordian fashion. Seated in a group, the children try to guess each picture as the teacher unfolds it a section at a time.

Finding Letters

When the children are studying a particular letter, give each of them a page from a magazine and a light colored marking or highlighting pen. Every time the subject letter appears on the magazine page, have the child mark through it. For example, if the letter is "B" the child should mark through all the "b's" on his or her page. If desired, staple each child's page to a piece of construction paper to give it importance.

Matching Facial Expressions

Prepare two identical sets of 5" × 6" face cards. Vary the faces by altering the position of eyes, mouth, etc. If possible, laminate the cards for increased durability. Shuffle the cards and let the children take turns matching the pairs of faces.[1]

[1]Similar to "Early Stages," manufactured by James Galt and Company, Ltd., Brookfield Road, Cheadle, Chesire, England.

Teacher Made Matching Exercises

Matching exercises are easy to construct and may be used to reinforce initial learning experiences. Draw rows of objects. Include a given stimulus which is also drawn in a box at the beginning of each row. The figure in the box is to be found by the child in the row of objects and circled. You may use shapes, letters, numerals or words.

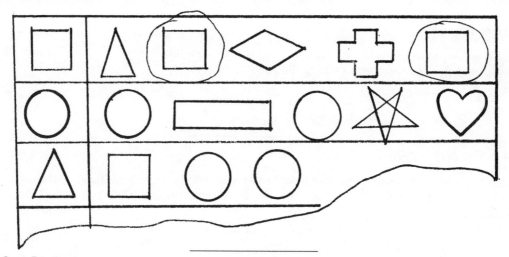

My Own Dictionary

Give the children books the pages of which are blank except for the printing of a single letter on the top of each page. The children may copy the letter or draw a picture of an object beginning with the same letter. Older children may write in as many words as they can think of which start with each letter on that letter's page.

Class Dictionary

Prepare twenty-six pages by printing one letter of the alphabet at the top of each page. Let the children select a page and draw one or more objects on the page beginning with the letter on the top of their page. Clip the pages together to make a class book for the classroom bookshelf.

Excursion Booklets

After an excursion, ask the children to draw a picture of what they enjoyed most. Either the teacher or the student labels each picture. Staple the pictures together into a class booklet.

Folded Names

Print each child's name with a black felt tipped pen on the end of a strip of typing paper. Fold the other end of the strip over the name so that the name is covered. Children trace their own names on the top of the folded strip with pencil.

Letter Patterns

There are four basic letter shapes used in many children's books:

    o dots   ı short sticks

    ʝ looped sticks   **l** long sticks[1]

Using this information, teachers can design exercises and activities to teach pattern recognition of letters. Some suggestions are:

1. Using a felt board and felt shapes (dots and sticks) children arrange letters by following a pattern.

2. Using colored paper dots and sticks, children follow directions to form letters by placing sticks in front of dots, in back of dots, etc.

3. Children complete worksheets which require them to find and match letters or words.

Letter Puzzles

Print upper and lower case letters on 3" × 5" cards. Cut each card in half in a unique pattern. No two letters should be cut alike. Children match the halves together.

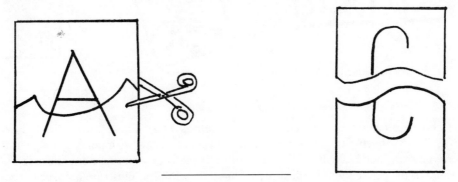

---

[1]Montgomery, Diane, "Teaching Prereading Skills through Training in Pattern Recognition," from *The Reading Teacher*, Vol. 30, No. 6 (March 1977). International Reading Association.

Finding Letters

The following exercise can be used as a chalkboard game with one or two players or as a worksheet for individual children. The teacher draws the figure shown here and asks the children to find as many capital letters as possible in it. Spend some time with the child introducing him to the activity before letting him explore it on his own.

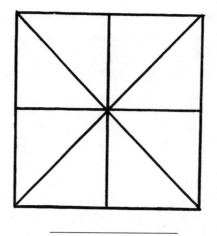

Puzzles of Paintings

Gather large pictures of famous paintings and laminate them to various colored poster boards. Using a different colored backing on each picture makes it easy to keep the pictures separate. Cut the pictures into puzzles for the children to put together.

Matching Snowflakes

The teacher draws matching pairs of snowflake patterns on typing paper and mounts them on posterboard. They may be laminated for durability. Children take turns matching them.

Cooperative Books

Read the children a familiar fairy tale or story such as "The Three Little Pigs." Then give the children 12" × 18" sheets of manila paper and tell them to draw with pencils the part of the story they enjoyed most. Then have the children color their pictures with crayon. Label each picture and arrange them in proper sequence. Illustrate or have the children illustrate a cover on posterboard. Assemble the pages and cover into a book and secure them together with brads. Keep the book on the classroom bookshelf for student use.

Vocabulary Lists

When Sylvia Ashton-Warner was teaching the Maori children in New Zealand, she realized that the first words introduced to beginning readers were neither meaningful nor interesting to them. Maori children didn't relate to the usual "Look, Sally, look" stories. She was determined to inject life into their vocabularies and allow children to select words relevant to them. Her method consisted of making a key vocabulary for each child from his immediate environment in order to build up an organic reading list for the class.

Ms. Ashton-Warner asked each child to tell her the word he or she wanted to learn to read that week. Using 5" × 12" tagboard cards and a black marker, she wrote the word and gave the card to the child who was allowed to work with it in school and take it home that night. The children brought back the cards the next day and put them in a large box. Each morning Ms. Ashton-Warner tipped the cards out of the box and each child found his or her own word. With a partner, the children read and taught each other their own word. She had the children learn a new word each week.[1]

If teachers are receptive to this idea it can be successful with children of any age. Two copies of each word should be made, one copy for the child to take home and keep and the other (laminated) for the teacher to keep permanently in the classroom.

Visual Grouping of Letters or Words

This exercise provides practice in the visual discrimination of words containing similarities. Write two or three pairs of words on the chalkboard. One child at a time points out the differences in the pairs. Examples:

| kitten | run | bus | sled | no | hit | messy |
| mitten | ran | bun | sleep | on | bit | mossy |

March Around the Alphabet

Make alphabet cards by printing single letters on pieces of manila paper. Place the alphabet cards in a large circle on the floor. The children march around them. When the teacher rings a bell or blows a whistle, each child picks up the nearest card and the children take turns identifying the letter on their card. Those who cannot identify the letter on the card they hold are out of the game.

Variation: Instead of alphabet cards, use word cards. This game will reinforce the children's reading program.

Pegboard Game With Dice

Make two dice from wooden blocks or cubes. Paint the numerals 1-6 on one; paint the other with the colors of the pegs of the classroom pegboard set. Two children play at a time using two pegboards, the dice and various colored pegs. The children take turns rolling the dice and fill up their pegboards according to the roll of the dice. For instance, if the color blue turns up on one die and the numeral 4 on the other, the child adds four blue pegs to his pegboard. The first one to fill his or her board wins.

---

[1]Ashton-Warner, Sylvia, *Teacher.* New York: Simon and Schuster, 1963, pp. 33-52.

Command Cards

This kind of task has been used successfully in Montessori schools for many years. Write simple command words on tagboard and keep the tags in a basket. Two or more children may play. The children take turns picking a card and obeying the command. After obeying the command, the child shows the tag to the other child or children playing and they decide if he or she followed the directions correctly.

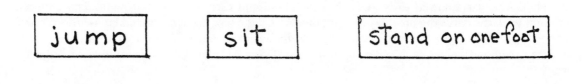

Go Fish

Cut out a large number of posterboard fish and put a paper clip on each one so that they will respond to a magnet. Use a toy fishing rod or three foot length of bamboo with a string attached. Tie a magnet to the end of the string. Print a numeral or a letter or a word on each fish. Children take turns fishing the paper fish out of a plastic basket. When a child catches a fish, he or she must read the word in order to keep the fish. At the end of the game, the child who has the most fish wins.

Dominoes

Make a set of twenty-six or more domino cards from posterboard. Draw a line down the middle of each domino and draw a single object or figure on each half of the domino. Both objects or figures may be the same. Traditionally, dominoes contain the familiar pattern of dots. You can use any number of ideas for the figures on the domino cards, however. For instance, you can make domino sets using words, animals, food, traffic signs, automobiles and machines, or make finish-the-picture and match-mother-with-the-baby dominoes. Even dominoes made from a variety of wallpaper patterns make an absorbing game. Old wallpaper books are usually available at no cost. You might make one set with dots and one with numerals and have the children match dots to numerals. Generally, you should use no more than seven or eight different objects or patterns in one set of dominoes so that you achieve a sufficient repetition of the patterns.

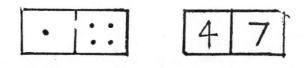

Method of play is simple. Divide the pile of domino cards between two players. The first player places one domino face up on the table. The second player must match one side of the domino with one of his own or lose a turn. The first child to play all his dominoes wins.

Lotto

Lotto games may be made or purchased. They are usually designed to be played by four to six children at a time. Each child has a playing card with several objects drawn on it. The caller (either the teacher or one of the children) picks one card from a pack of caller cards, each of which is a reproduction of one of the pictures contained on the larger playing cards. The child whose playing card has the object pictured on the card the caller picks covers the object on his playing card with the matching smaller card. The first child to cover all the objects on his or her card wins. The caller may be instructed to play the game in one of several ways:

1. Hold up the card and call the name of the object.
2. Call out the name of the object without showing the small card.
3. Show the small card without calling out the name of the object.

Use a variety of subjects, such as food, occupations, cooking utensils, toys, sports, animals, plants, verbs (running, jumping, falling, etc.), prepositions (in, on, under, over, etc.), clothing or seasons. Make sure that all the objects pictured in a set are related in some way. Examples are:

Games similar to these were designed by Dr. Lasar Gotkin to increase vocabulary and strengthen language skills, and to encourage interdependence between pupils while lessening dependence on the teacher.[1]

---

[1]Gotkin, Lassar, *Language Lotto Games,* Appleton-Century-Croft

Experience Charts

Experience charts, when properly used, expose children to the relationship between the spoken and written word. The teacher elicits ideas from students and writes them on the chart tablet as the children speak. Charts may be composed of words or illustrations or combination of both, depending on the developmental level of the children. Use experience charts in cooperative planning by the students, such as discussing what to expect to see on a field trip or deciding what songs to sing for a school program. You may also use the chart tablet to enhance unit work through listing. For example, you can make lists of occupations, ways of traveling, classroom rules, favorite toys, favorite sports, etc. In addition, you may use experience charts for special experiences, such as recording recipes, dictating letters to government officials, or describing unusual natural phenomenon. Be sure that the chosen subject is one which will stimulate student responses and contributions. For the pre-reading crowd, repetition of words is desirable since it facilitates recognition. For emphasis, often used words may be printed in a different color from the body of the composition. When the chart is finished, the children may take turns reading some or all of the words.

Use of Color in Teaching Letters

The Montessori system teaches with a moveable alphabet that assigns one color to vowels and another color to consonants. When taught with this alphabet, children begin to differentiate between the two kinds of letters. In addition, as children begin to formulate words with the moveable alphabet, they learn that every word contains at least one vowel, which is easily recognizable by its color.

Sequence Worksheet

The teacher draws simple pictures of a series of events which are not in their natural sequence. Children color the pictures, cut them out, and paste them in their proper order.

Sequence Cards

The teacher pastes a series of magazine pictures or a sequential comic strip on posterboard cards and lamnates them for durability. Children take turns arranging them in order and reading them to the teacher or to fellow students.

Sequence With Beads

Attach a row of beads securely with staples to the upper half of a heavy cardboard card (approximately 8" × 4"). Secure one end of an empty lace below the row of beads. The child copies the pattern of the completed row of beads by threading loose beads on the empty lace.

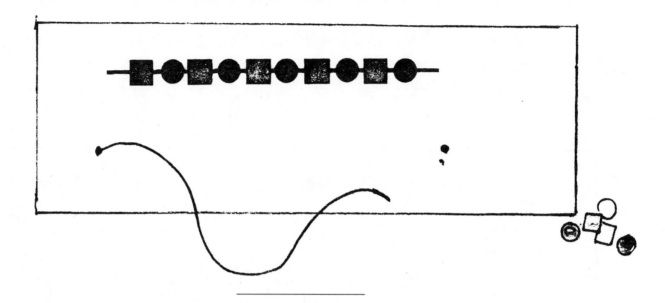

The model pictured above contains beads of one color in two alternating shapes. The teacher can make more difficult patterns by using more than two shapes, two or more colors, or a combination of different shapes and different colors.[1]

Simple Sequence Cards

The teacher draws a series of simple pictures on posterboard cards. The first picture is a simple design made up of several components. The second picture is a repeat of the first, except that when drawing the second picture, the teacher omits one component of the original design. In the third picture, the teacher repeats the second picture but omits another component. The teacher continues making the series of pictures until the final picture contains just a single feature or component of the original design. Children take turns arranging the series in order—either by adding features or subtracting them.

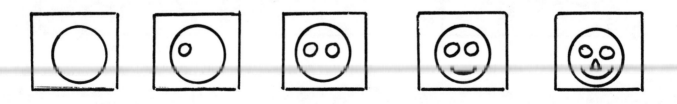

[1]Exercises similar to this one were introduced in the publication: Wilson, John A. R. and Robeck, Mildred C., *Kindergarten Evaluation of Learning Potential,* McGraw-Hill, 1963.

D. PRE-WRITING

The ability to write stems from fundamental multi-sensory and motor development activities. These exercises amplify eye-hand coordination which is essential for holding and guiding a pencil and forming letters.

No undue pressure should be applied to the child in the early classes. Neatness and accuracy are secondary. The primary concerns are encouraging the child to participate, introducing stimulating activities, and allowing individually paced advancement.

The use of crayons, pencils, scissors, paste, rulers, clay, puzzles, pegs, painting, sewing cards, small blocks and logs, chalkboard exploration and finger plays can be used to promote eye-hand coordination. In addition, try the following ideas:

Writing Table

In a quiet area of the room, set up a special writing table with lined or plain paper and pencils. In addition, the teacher may supply different accessories to heighten student interest, such as:

> Rulers
> Letter stencils to trace
> A box full of words to copy
> Blank books
> Worksheets which promote writing
> Tracing boards
> Tracing paper

Tracing Boards

Draw a repeating pattern or print a series of letters on strips of posterboard. Laminate each strip. Children use soft wax crayons to trace over the design or the letters and then wipe the crayon off with a tissue.

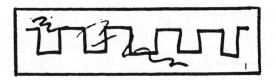

Use of a Shape Board

Construct shape boards—similar to those used by optometrists—out of heavy cardboard. Children may trace the shapes pictured on the board on manila paper and then color them or they may trace the shapes on colored construction paper and cut them out. Either method is an exercise in small motor development.

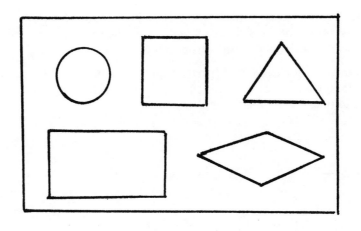

Copying Words

Give the children lined sheets of typing paper with their names or other familiar words (stop, go, slow, yes, no, etc.) printed in large letters across the top. Have the children copy each letter in each word on every line.

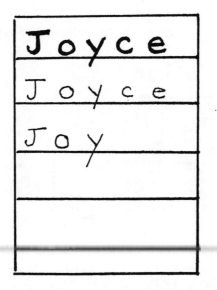

Worksheets

The teacher draws the beginning of a pattern on each line of a sheet of lined paper and has the children finish each pattern to the end of the line. Patterns may be mimeographed on the paper or drawn with felt marking pens.

The following two ideas come from British Infant or Primary Schools.

Rebus Story

Children make up their own stories using a combination of pictures and words. Simple drawings are acceptable. Nursery rhymes or familiar fairy tales may also be subjects.

Blank Books

Prepare blank booklets from typing paper or lined school tablet paper to be used on the writing table. Make the covers from colored construction paper. Make the books in creative shapes to encourage creative writing. Let the children fill the pages of the books as they wish.

Bulletin Board

Make a large umbrella out of posterboard and draw the alphabet on it, as shown below. Tack the umbrella on the bulletin board. Cut out a large number of raindrops from construction paper. Have the children print a letter on each raindrop and tack the raindrop onto the matching letter on the umbrella. If the younger children don't tack the raindrops in the proper place it makes it appear to be raining, so all efforts are acceptable.

Worksheets

The following are two pre-writing worksheets which help develop eye-hand coordination.

Copy the drawing

Color the square. Use a pencil and draw many larger squares around it.*

*NOTE: You can make similar sheets using a triangle, circle, rectangle, etc.
_____

Connect the Dots

Paul McKee asserts that there are ten common words which make up about one fourth of all printed English. Giving the kindergarten child practice in tracing these letters so that he learns to recognize them will work to the child's advantage when he begins first grade work. The ten words are:

a, I, in, is, it, of, to, the, and, that[1]

Prepare worksheets of these words such as the one pictured below and instruct the children to connect the dots, then write the word.

name _____

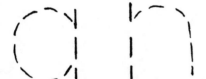

[1]From *Reading, A Program of Instruction for Pre-Elementary School,* by Paul McKee. Copyright © 1966 by Houghton Mifflin Company. Used with permission.

Fill in the Missing Letter

Another type of worksheet using the common words has two columns. The model column is complete and the second has missing letters which the children supply by copying the word in the model column.

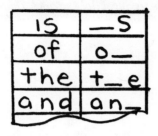

E. SPELLING

The most desirable spelling lists for children in the primary grades are organically developed. Words may come from the children's vocabularies, social studies texts, arithmetic problems, objects in the classroom, songs, holidays, stories, etc. Many of the exercises already given in this chapter promote spelling concepts along with other skills. The following activities, however, are designed primarily with spelling in mind.

Copying the Words

Ask the children to copy a spelling list in manuscript and then in cursive writing.

Stories

Have the children make up a story using as many spelling words as possible. The story should make sense.

Initial Sounds and Root Phrases

Construct worksheets by drawing the stem and center of one or more flowers. In each flower's center print a root phrase. Have the children draw petals around the flower centers and print in each petal an initial letter which, when combined with the root phrase, spells a word.

Autograph Books

The teacher prepares blank booklets for each child by stapling three or four sheets of lined writing paper to the inside of a 9" × 12" piece of construction paper folded in half. Children collect autographs of their classmates during work period, then read their collection to the teacher.

Word Jumbles

The Suder Elementary School experiment in Jonesboro, Georgia, sponsored by the Georgia Department of Education and the University of Georgia, used the following exercise in the pre-kindergarten/kindergarten classes:

A basket of words printed on individual pieces of oak tag were kept on a table. Children selected a word that they wanted to learn and took it to the teacher. The teacher cut the word up into individual letters. The child then arranged the letters in their proper order.

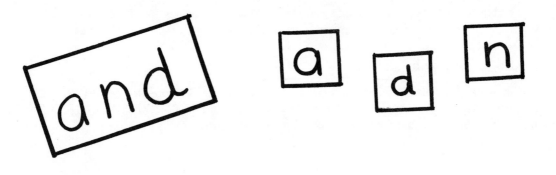

Tic Tac Toe Spelling Game

Children choose partners to play. Of each pair, one child decides to be X and the other O. The teacher calls a word for the X's. They write it down and show it to their partner. Then the teacher writes it on the chalkboard. If the child has spelled the word correctly, he or she places an "X" on the tic tac toe grill he or she is playing with his or her partner. The next spelling word is directed to the O's. The children play tic tac toe by the regular rules when they "win" the right to take a turn by spelling a word correctly.

Verbs

Give each child a blank book, scissors and old magazines. Have the children cut out action pictures from the magazines and paste each picture on a page of the blank book. Help each child describe each picture and write the descriptive verb below it on the page.

Compound Words

The teacher prepares a set of picture cards. Print the name of the object pictured on the back of each card. Children put the cards together to form compound words. When a child has gained competency in this activity, he or she can arrange the words without looking at the picture. Examples of words to be used are: bird, house, rain, bow, sun, light, back, fire, fly.

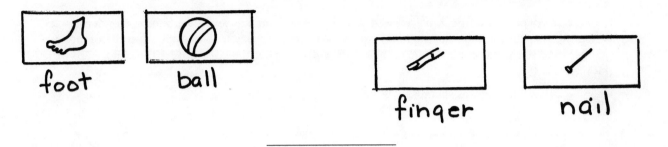

Match and Spell

The teacher writes a short paragraph on the chalkboard composed of as many words as there are children in the class. Give each child a card containing one of the words in the paragraph. The children take turns sticking their word over the matching word in the paragraph with tape, spelling the word out loud at the same time. Soon the paragraph will be covered entirely.

F. POETRY

When exposed to poetry, children develop a sense of rhyming and rhyming words which are a basic part of reading instruction at the same time they are learning to appreciate poetry's beauty and charm. When children read "hat, cat, bat, rat," etc., they are in fact rhyming by using several initial consonants with a single root phrase.

A variety of emotions can be released through poems, such as joy, love, humor, wonderment, suspense, amazement, bewilderment and sadness. The teacher may wish to display a series of mood pictures and suggest a simple rhyme to the children, leaving out the last word for the children to fil' in. Example:

> "The sun was shining so very bright
> I didn't have to turn on the _____."

Some of the most appropriate poems for young children are listed here.

1. Animal Poems

Mice

I think mice
Are rather nice.

Their tails are long,
Their faces small,
They haven't any
Chins at all.
Their ears are pink
Their teeth are white,
They run about
The house at night.
They nibble things
They shouldn't touch
And no one seems
To like them much.

But I think mice
Are nice.

Rose Fyleman[1]

[1]From *Fifty-one New Nursery Rhymes,* by Rose Fyleman. Copyright © 1931, 1932 by Doubleday & Company, Inc.

Good Morning

One day I saw a downy duck,
With feathers on his back;
I said, "Good morning downy duck,"
And he said, "Quack, quack, quack."

One day I saw a timid mouse,
He was so shy and meek;
I said, "Good morning, timid mouse,"
And he said, "Squeak, squeak, squeak."

One day I saw a curly dog,
I met him with a bow;
I said, "Good morning, curly dog,"
And he said, "Bow-wow-wow."

One day I saw a scarlet bird,
He woke me from my sleep;
I said, "Good morning, scarlet bird,"
And he said, "Cheep, cheep, cheep."
Muriel Sipe

The Little Turtle

There was a little turtle.
He lived in a box.
He swam in a puddle.
He climbed on the rocks.

He snapped at a mosquito.
He snapped at a flea.
He snapped at a minnow.
And he snapped at me.

He caught the mosquito.
He caught the flea.
He caught the minnow.
But he didn't catch me.
Vachel Lindsay

Reprinted with permission of MacMillan Publishing Co., Inc. from *Collected Poems* by Vachel Lindsay. Copyright © 1920 by MacMillan Publishing Co., Inc., renewed 1948 by Elizabeth C. Lindsay.

Thanksgiving

I have a turkey big and fat,
He spread his tail and walks like that.
His daily corn he would not miss,
And when he talks he sound like this:
Gobble, gobble, gobble!
Unknown

2. Seasons and Weather

Spring

The days are getting warmer
I know it must be spring.
I saw some pussy-willows;
I heard a robin sing.
Unknown

The Seasons

Summer, winter, spring, and fall
How we love them one and all.
Each one brings us lots of fun
Rain and snow, and nice warm sun.

Unknown

Fog

The fog comes on
little cat feet.

It sits looking
over harbor and city
on silent haunches
and then moves on.

Carl Sandburg

Little Wind

Little wind, blow on the hill-top;
Little wind, blow down the plain;
Little wind, blow up the sunshine,
Little wind, blow off the rain.

Kate Greenaway

Rain

The rain is raining all around,
  It falls on field and tree,
It rains on the umbrellas here,
And on the ships at sea.

Robert Louis Stevenson

3. People

I Never Hear

I never hear my mother come
Into my room late late at night.
She says she has to look and see
If I'm still tucked exactly right.
Nor do I feel her kissing me.
She says she does, though.
Every night.

Dorothy Aldis[1]

Growing Up

My birthday is coming tomorrow,
And then I'm going to be four;
And I'm getting so big that already,
I can open the kitchen door;
I'm very much taller than Baby,
Though today I am still only three;
And I'm bigger than Bob-tail the puppy,
Who used to be bigger than me.

Unknown

Five Years Old

Please, everybody, look at me!
Today I'm five years old you see!
And after this I won't be four
Not ever, ever, any more!
I won't be 3 or 2 or 1
For that was when I'd first begun.
Now I'll be five a while and then
I'll soon be something else again!

Mary Louise Allen[2]

4. Guessing Poems

Who Am I

Whisky, frisky
Hippity, hop,
Up he goes to the treep top!
Whirly, twirly, round and round,
Down he scampers to the ground.
Furly, curly what a tail
Tall as a feather, broad as a sail!
Where's his supper? In a shell,
Snappy, cracky, out it fell!

Unknown

Riddle: What Am I?

They chose me from my brothers:
"That's the nicest one," they said,
And they carved me out a face and put a
Candle in my head;
And they set me on the doorstep.
Oh, the night was dark and wild;
But when they lit the candle,
Then I smiled.

Dorothy Aldis[1]

What Is It?

Tall ears,
Twinkly nose,
Tiny tail,
And—hop he goes!

What is he—
Can you guess?
I feed him carrots
And watercress

His ears are long,
His tail is small—
And he doesn't make any
Noise at all!

Tall ears,
Twinkly nose,
Tiny tail,
And—hop, he goes!

Mary Louise Allen[2]

[1]Reprinted by permission of G. P. Putnam's Sons from *Hop, Skip & Jump* by Dorothy Aldis. Copyright 1934; renewed © 1961 by Dorothy Aldis.

[2]The text of "What Is It?" from *A Pocketful of Poems* by Marie Louise Allen. Text copyright © 1957 by Marie Allen Howarth. Originally appeared in *A Pocketful of Rhymes* by the same author. By permission of Harper & Row, Publishers, Inc.

Guessing Games Involving Poetry and Fairy Tales

Ask the children, "What would happen if . . . ?"

- Little Miss Muffet liked spiders?
- Goldilock's brother came to find her?
- Mary's little lamb got lost while he was following her to school?
- the prince who ran after Cinderella stepped on the glass slipper and broke it to pieces?
- there was a hole in Jack and Jill's bucket?
- the seven dwarfs didn't like Snow White and chased her away?
- the big bad wolf had a bad cold and he couldn't huff and puff?
- the giant climbed down to the bottom of the beanstalk?
- Big Brother Billy Goat Gruff didn't cross the bridge?
- after Pinocchio ran away, Geppeto made himself another puppet and Geppeto liked the new one better because it didn't tell lies?

Prepare and ask other provocative questions and encourage the children to think of "what if" questions also.

———————————

Great changes have occurred in the field of mathematics during the last fifty years. Because of these changes, new teaching methods have evolved which can be adapted into programs for the very young child.

The traditional "telling and drilling" instruction has been replaced largely by informal presentations which promote active student participation. Emphasis is placed on self-discovery through illustrations, tactile demonstrations, group projects, cooperative games, and individualized work. Children learn to compare and observe quantity, size, weight, values of exchanges, degree and time. In addition, efforts are made to integrate the program with the environment by using natural materials such as rocks, shells, leaves, sand, water, and snow whenever possible.

In addition to planned activities, a teacher can use spontaneous teaching "spots." For example, when a child is asked to take two cookies or to break a cookie in half, he or she is learning elementary numerical concepts.

A. VOCABULARY

Use words that have mathematical significance when presenting mathematical concepts to young children. Because learning is continuous and developmental, children should be exposed both to mathematical terms and their symbols:

plus	$+$
minus	$-$
equals	$=$
doesn't equal	$\neq$
greater than	$>$
less than	$<$

Terms of comparison

few	fewer	fewest
large	larger	largest
long	longer	longest
short	shorter	shortest
fat	fatter	fattest
small	smaller	smallest
tall	taller	tallest
wide	wider	widest

General Vocabulary

above	fast	many	same
add	first	match	set
after	heavy	member	shape
alike	high	money	short
before	hour	more	side
between	inside	most	size
big	large	narrow	slow
bottom	last	next	small
connect	length	number	straight
cost	less	numeral	symbol
count	light	one-to-one	through
curve	like	order	time
curved	line	outside	top
different	little	over	under
dot	long	point	value
enough	low	row	wide

B. NUMERALS AND NUMBERS

The teacher must understand the terms "number" and "numeral" and use them properly. "Number" stands for an abstract amount while "numeral" is the name for the written symbol.

1. Numerals

The Telephone

The teacher provides an extension telephone to be used for free exploration by the children. Usually the telephone company will donate used telephone to schools.

Telephone Directories

Make the children blank booklets by stapling small sheets of paper to the inside of a folded piece of 8½" × 11" construction paper. Give the children the blank booklets. Have the children collect the names and telephone numbers of their classmates and write them in their booklets.

Or list all the children's names and telephone numbers on a chart tablet and have the children copy them in their directories.

Telephone Bulletin Board

Staple a light shade of colored construction paper over the entire surface of a bulletin board. Draw a large telephone in the center. Cut the receiver and the dialing surface out of posterboard and tack them to the board. Children then take turns dialing their own telephone number.

In addition, provide the children with the receiver pattern. Have each child trace and cut out a receiver and write his or her name and telephone number on it. Tack the receivers to the bulletin board.

thumb/tack

Sandpaper Numerals

Sandpaper letters and numerals were first introduced into schools by Maria Montessori. They can be purchased in school supply houses or constructed by the teacher. Cut out three inch numerals from sandpaper and mount them on 4" × 4" cards. The cards provide tactile stimulation while teaching numeral configuration. Children enjoy using them with blindfolds, first feeling and then saying the numeral out loud.

House Numerals

The teacher tacks a long sheet of wrapping paper to the bulletin board and draws a road along the bottom. Have the children draw their houses or apartments and write their name and house number on them. The children then cut them out and tack them on the road. The children may then add people, animals, trees, flowers, etc., to the bulletin board scene.

Tracing Numerals

Print large numerals on long strips of white posterboard. Cover the strips with clear contact paper or laminate them. Children trace the numerals with crayons and erase the crayon with soft tissue.

Matching Numerals

The teacher marks ten squares each in the bottom of empty stocking boxes and prints the numerals from 1 to 10 in the squares. Paste or print matching numerals on small squares of colored construction paper. (An old calendar can provide many numerals.) Children take turns matching the small cards to the numerals in the box.

Copying Numerals

The teacher prepares lined worksheets. Draw a box at the beginning of each line and print a numeral in it. The children are to copy the numeral in each box in the adjoining blank space. Duplicate the worksheets on a duplicating machine so that each child will have one to work.

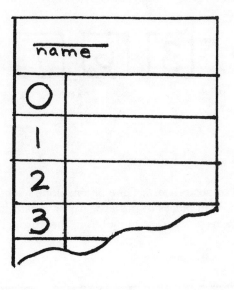

Clock Sequence

The teacher constructs a large clock out of posterboard and cuts out the numerals. The teacher gives the child twelve discs, labelled from 1 to 12, to fit into the proper spaces.

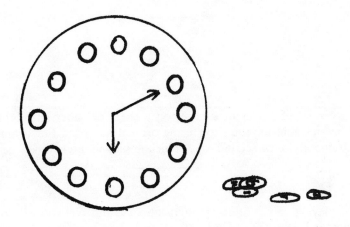

Sequence Cards

Display ten cards of numerals to a group of children. Have them hide their eyes and then remove one or more card(s). Then have the children open their eyes and guess which numeral(s) is missing. In addition, the teacher can make deliberate errors in sequence and have the children point out the mistake. Example:

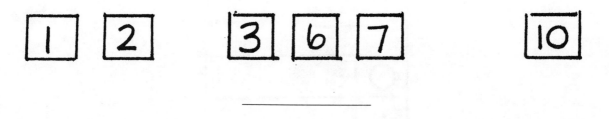

Sequence Cards

Draw ten squares on a piece of posterboard. Glue an envelope to the bottom of the posterboard. Print the numerals 1 to 10 on small pieces of posterboard or construction paper and store them in the envelope. Children take turns placing the numerals in their proper order on the squares.

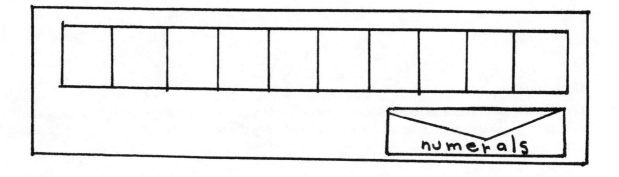

2. Numbers

Ordinal Numbers

Draw four or five rows of circles or squares on a sheet of paper and duplicate the sheet. Give children directions for coloring the sheet using ordinal numbers. For example, "In the first row, color the first circle red. In the second row, color the second circle blue."

Bulletin Board of Familiar Numbers

Tack calendars, playing cards, rulers, grocery checks, and pictures of clocks, telephones, mail boxes, thermometers, license tags, scales, etc., on the board. In addition, you may have the children write numbers and tack them on the board.

Matching

Draw ten squares on a large sheet of posterboard. Number the squares from one to ten using dots (as from dominoes) instead of numerals. Prepare a set of matching dot cards plus a set of number cards. Children take turns matching the dots and numbers to the proper space on the board.

Matching Buttons to Numbers

Prepare ten number cards by printing the numerals 1 through 10 on ten index cards. Provide the children with a box of buttons or bottle caps. Have the children place the proper number of buttons or caps on each card.

Matching Numbers to Buttons

Sew a series of buttons on ten cloth strips. Sew one button on the first strip, two buttons on the second strip, etc. Staple each cloth strip to a separate piece of posterboard. Provide the children with a set of number cards (1-10) and have them match each button card to the correct number card.

Matching Configuration Cards

The teacher prepares a set of number cards from 0 to 10, a set of cards containing the number words zero to ten, and a set of dotted cards (like dominoes) from 0 to 10, out of thirty-three 6" × 8" oak tag rectangles. The cards may be color coded for very young children so that all ones are yellow, all twos are blue, etc. Children separate the cards into eleven piles, matching the symbols for each number.

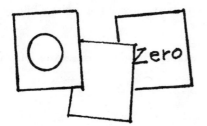

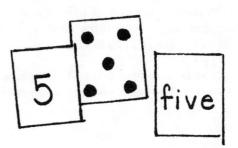

Wake Up Counting Game

The children close their eyes. They pretend to sleep. The teacher taps a ruler several times on a desk and says that it is time to get up. Then the children open their eyes and tell the teacher what time it is by the number of taps they heard.

Counting Game with Bean Bags

Tape a large square (2' × 2') on the floor with masking tape. Tape a base line on the floor, parallel to one side of the square but several feet away from it. Children take turns tossing a bean bag from the base line into the square. They count the number of times they succeed. When a child misses, it is the next child's turn. The teacher or the children may keep a tally count, if desired.

Different Ways to Write a Number

One often sees this project in the British Infant Schools. Provide the children with a roll of paper or a long strip of paper. Each child selects a number and discovers how many ways he or she can represent it.

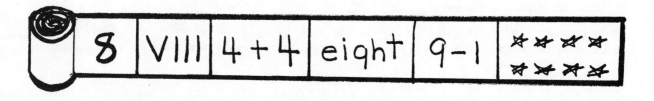

Class Discussion on Infinity

Introduce children to the concept of infinity. Have children address the question, Can infinity be counted? To help illustrate the concept of infinity, have the children count the grains of sand in a bucket of sand or the raindrops during a shower. Ask the children to think of other ideas which might represent infinity.

Odd and Even Numbers

Montessori schools use this kind of mathematical exercise effectively. Give children number cards (1-10) and fifty-five discs (or buttons or chips). The children arrange the cards in order and under each number they arrange pairs of discs corresponding to the number indicated on the card. A child can determine odd or even numbers from the results: even numbers show equal pairs while odd numbers have an extra disc.

The game is self-correcting if the teacher gives the children exactly fifty-five discs. Any leftover discs or a shortage of discs signify an error.

Counting Game

Children are seated in a circle. The teacher or a child begins the counting by saying, "one." The next child says, "two," etc., until the circle is complete and all have called out a number.

Number Worksheet

Prepare a worksheet on graph paper. In the first box of each row of squares, print a number. Have the children color in the number of squares in each row indicated by the number in the first box.

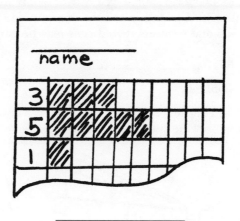

Number Chart

Draw 110 squares on a large square piece of posterboard: eleven squares across and ten squares down. Write the number 1-10 down the first column. Provide the children a box of chips, buttons, bottle caps, discs or small pieces of paper. Children place the corresponding number of chips (or buttons, etc.) next to each number on the chart.

Counting

The teacher listens to each child count to 100 by 1's and 10's while using an abacus. Older children may count by 2's, 5's, etc.

C. ONE-TO-ONE CORRESPONDENCE

One-to-One in Cans

This is an exercise similar to Montessori's spindle box. Cover empty frozen juice cans with contact paper and label them from 0 to 10. Children place the appropriate number of popsicle sticks or coffee stirrers in each can. Odd and even numbered cans may be covered with different colored paper.

One-to-One Correspondence Booklets

Fold three sheets of paper in half and staple them together on the center fold. Write a number on the top of each page. Children draw or cut out and paste pictures to match the number on each page.

One-to-One Correspondence with Hole Punchers

Draw ten shapes on a piece of tag board. Number each shape from 1 to 10. Provide children with paper squares and a hole puncher. The children punch a number of holes in each paper square and place the square on the numbered shape on the tagboard which matches the number of holes.

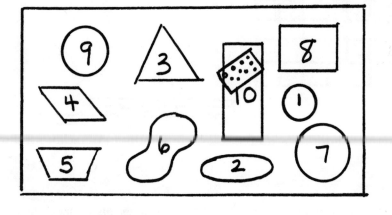

One-to-One Correspondence on the Bulletin Board

The teacher folds in half ten pieces of 8½" × 12" construction paper in a variety of colors. On the outside half of each sheet, draw a number of shapes (stars, dots, bars, etc.). Write the corresponding number on the inside of each sheet. Tack the folded sheets on the bulletin board. Children take turns counting the figures to come up with the matching number. They can check their answers by lifting the paper and reading the number. If desired, attach a sign up sheet to the bulletin board for those children who have completed reading all the numbers to sign.

One-to-One Correspondence with Felt Trees

This activity has proved successful in Head Start Programs.

Prepare ten numbered tree cards. Make the tree tops from green felt and paint the trunks with brown paint. Write a number under each tree. Then make a large number of red felt apples to accompany the tree cards. Children attach the number of apples to each tree to match the number under the tree.

One-to-One Correspondence with Ladybugs

Cut out eleven circles from red posterboard. With marking pens, draw a different number of dots on each circle. Make eleven heads and number them from 0 to 10. If desired, attach pipe cleaners to the heads for antennae. The child matches each head to the body with the corresponding number of dots.

One-to-One Correspondence with Kites and Clothespins

Cut out several posterboard kites and print a number on each one. Attach a long string tail to each kite. Furnish the child with a box of clothespins. Have the child attach the correct number of clothespins to each tail to correspond with the number written on the kite.

One-to-One Correspondence with Coat Hangers

Cut out a number of cardboard circles and print a number on each one. Attach one cardboard circle in the middle of each hanger with scotch tape. Have the children attach the correct number of clothespins to the bottom of each hanger to correspond with the number written on the cardboard circle.

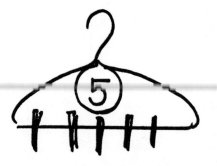

D. SETS

Sets are collections of things, such as checkers, crayons, shapes, wild animals, or farm animals. An important aspect in the study of sets is the ability of the child to grasp the unique qualities within a given group. The following exercises teach the concept of sets.

Bingo

Prepare bingo cards using the numerals 1-10. Arrange each card in four columns: red, white, blue and yellow. When playing, the caller names both a number and a color and the children must be able to identify a numeral in its correct color set in order to cover it.

———————

Color Sets

Cover a small table or desk with paper or cloth in a solid color. Display the name of the color nearby. Have the children bring things from home or find things during the school day in the classroom which are the same color and put them on the table. Select a different color each week.

———————

Spotting the Set[1]

Prepare large cards containing pictures of groups of sets. Make single matching sets on small cards. Place the small cards face down in the center of the table. Two, three, or four children may play. Each child has a large card. Players take turns picking small cards. If a small card matches a picture on the child's large card, the child keeps it and covers the corresponding picture on his large card. The winner is the child who covers his card first.

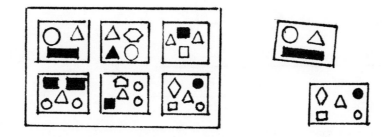

———————

———————

[1]This idea and the following two ideas for teaching sets are modeled after games contained in Galt's *Early Stages* catalogue which can be obtained by writing to James Galt & Co., Brookfield Road, Cheadle, Chesire, England.

Matching Sets

Use thirty or more geometric shapes to make the set combinations. Make a large playing board with sets drawn on it and make small matching cards. The child places the small cards in their proper position.

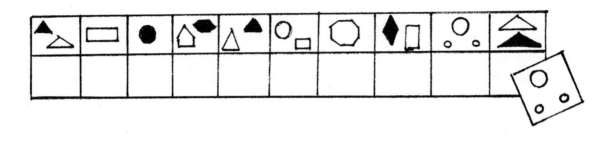

Sets Game

Give each child a large card with a picture made up of many geometric shapes drawn on it. Place matching geometric shapes in the center of the table. Children cover the picture on their card with appropriate shapes. This activity teaches children sets, subsets, union and intersection.

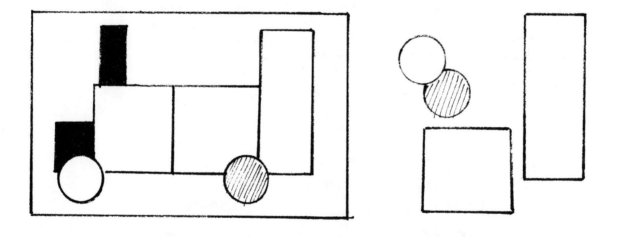

Picture Sets

The teacher cuts out and pastes on 3" × 5" cards many pictures of items belonging to two different sets. Examples are: fruits and vegetables, trees and flowers, numerals and letters. Mix up the cards and give them to the child. The child separates the pictures into their proper sets.

These cards can be used with children of all ages. Match the difficulty of the sets to the children's developmental level. For instance, older children might separate musical instruments into brass, woodwind and percussion sets.

For younger children, place boxes containing a picture representing each category next to the cards to assist the children in making judgments. For example, one box might show a picture of a farm while the other displays a jungle. Children then place farm animals in the farm box and wild animals in the jungle box.

Chalkboard Exercise with Intersecting Sets

Draw three or more overlapping shapes on the chalkboard. (For example, a triangle, a circle and a square.) Number each defined area. (See illustration below). Have the children sit in front of the chalkboard and ask them questions such as:

"What set of numerals is in the circle?"

"What set of numerals is in the square?"

"Which shape contains the numeral 2?"

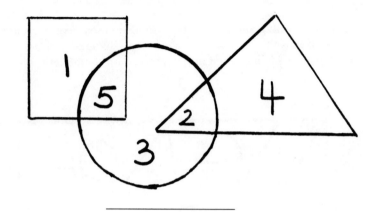

Sorting Box

This suggestion comes from the British Infant Schools.[1] Provide the child with a jar filled with buttons, bottle caps, shells, bolts, washers, toothpicks, etc., and a sorting box or several small boxes for sorting. The child examines the contents of the jar and sorts like objects into separate compartments or boxes.

[1]Nuffield Mathematics Project, *Mathematics Beings,* John Wiley & Sons, Inc., 1967.

E. GEOMETRIC SHAPES

Working with fundamental shapes introduces the child to geometrical concepts. Along with two dimensional figures, the child should be exposed to solid figures such as cubes, cones, cylinders, spheres, prisms, and pyramids.

Shape Bulletin Board

Fill an entire bulletin board with geometric shapes. Children then take turns identifying the various figures. Provide the children with equipment such as rulers, shape stencils and crayons, and let them make their own shape papers similar to the design created on the bulletin board.

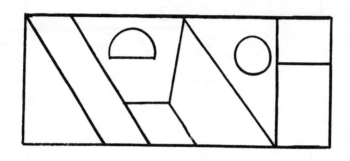

Matching Shapes

Prepare worksheets containing two rows of the same shapes in a different order. Children draw lines connecting like shapes.

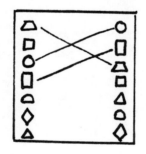

Printing Three Dimensional Shapes

The child presses the flat surface of a solid shape to a stamp pad or paints it with thick tempera, and then prints it on a sheet of paper. With this activity, children will begin to see a correlation between three dimensional figures and the two dimensional figures of which they are composed.

Mr. Shape Bulletin Board

Using triangles, squares, rectangles, a semi-circle and a trapezoid, the teacher constructs a bulletin board depicting a man holding a flower pot. (See illustration below.) Make a column of all the shapes used to make Mr. Shape along one side of the board. Tack a length of yarn to each shape in the column. Children then take turns connecting the piece of yarn attached to each shape in the column to the matching shape in Mr. Shape.

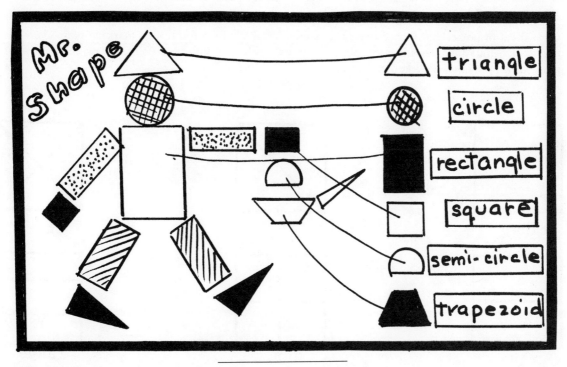

A Geoboard

Make a geoboard by hammering nails or pegs one inch apart on a 5" × 5" board, five rows across and five rows down. Use colored rubber bands to create patterns.

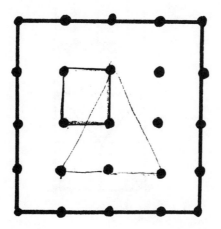

Matching Blocks

On a large white piece of vinyl, the teacher traces the outline of several kindergarten blocks. Or, the teacher may tape outlines directly onto an asphalt tile floor. Children place the corresponding block in the outline.

———————

Working with Shapes

On a sheet of posterboard trace twelve four inch squares with a felt tipped marking pen. Then cut out twelve four inch construction paper squares, each in a different color. Draw the following patterns on the construction paper squares.

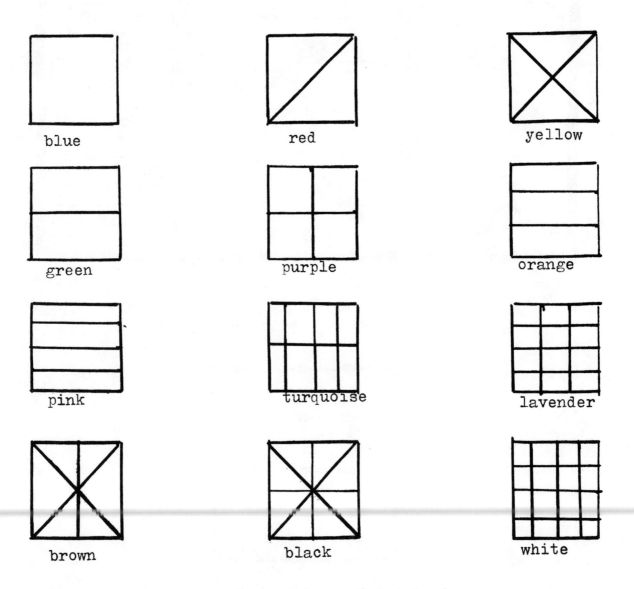

Children arrange these squares on the squares drawn on the posterboard.

———————

Shape Booklets

Prepare booklets in the shape of geometric figures. (For example, circles, squares, triangles, rectangles and ovals.) Children choose a booklet and on each page they draw pictures that contain the shape suggested by the book.

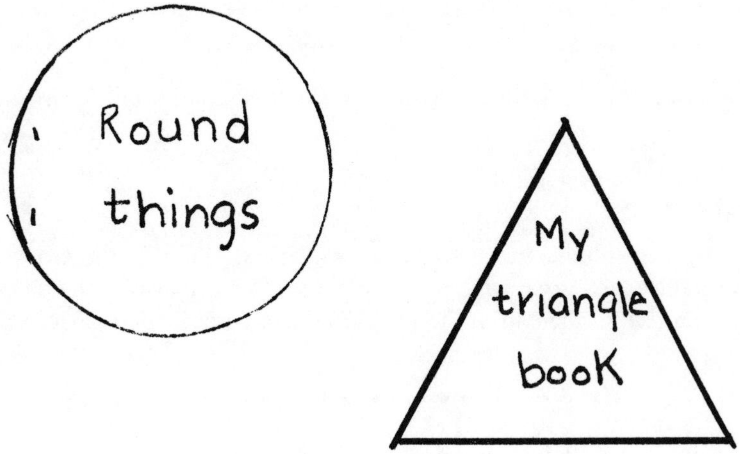

Round
things

My
triangle
book

F. PATTERNS

Pegboard Exercise

The teacher sets up a pattern on a sample peg board. Children copy the design on their own pegboards.

_____

Parquetry Blocks

Have children use parquetry blocks either to copy a pre-drawn pattern or to invent a design of their own.

_____

Finishing the Pattern

The teacher prepares finish-the-pattern worksheets. On each line of the worksheet the teacher establishes a pattern of shapes by drawing the first three or four figures in the pattern. The children are to continue the pattern to the end of the line. For more complicated patterns, include color.

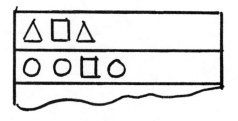

_____

G. MEASUREMENT

Measurement answers such questions as how much, how heavy, what time, how far and how long. It is an integral part of our daily lives. To the child, many areas of arithmetic may seem impractical, but measurement can be seen as a useful subject for study. The following activities are designed to teach children measurement concepts.

1. Linear Measurement

Rulers

Give each child a 12" strip of posterboard. The strip may include a head such as the one shown in the illustration. Using a ruler, the child marks off inches on the strip with a felt marking pen.

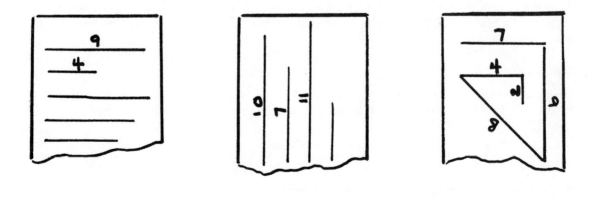

Worksheets

Teachers may devise various worksheets which contain exercises requiring the child to use a ruler. Kindergarten children work successfully with papers that require the measurement of inches; worksheets for children in the primary grades might include fractions. Examples:

Shoe Sizes

Children trace their shoes on colored construction paper, cut them out and measure them from heel to toe with a ruler. They record the measurement on the paper shoes.

Measurement Workbooks

The teacher staples two or three pieces of typing paper together between two pieces of construction paper. The child measures something in the schoolroom such as a desk, shelf, bookcase, piano, etc., and records the measurement on each page of the booklet. Children who can't write can draw a picture of the article.

Measuring Game

Children participate in broad jump exercises in the classroom. They measure their jumps and record them on a chart. A beanbag toss or ball toss can also be measured and recorded.

Measuring Plant Growth

Children keep a weekly record of the height of a potted plant in the classroom.

Task Cards

Task cards are often used in the British Infant Schools. Each card contains a job to be done by the child. Let the children take turns drawing cards from a box or basket and performing the tasks they call for. Examples:

>   With a partner, measure the perimeter of the room.
>   With a partner, measure the perimeter of the school.
>   Measure the teacher's desk.
>   Measure the front door to the room.
>   Figure out how many 12" rulers fit together to make a yardstick.

---

2. Time

Comparative Timers

Exhibit a collection of timers (for example, a watch, alarm clock, egg timer, stop watch, and an hour glass) on the arithmetic table. Let the children use two or three at the same time to observe if they are synchronized.

Calendars

Give the children twelve seasonal pictures plus a set of index cards containing the names of the twelve months. Children try to match the season with the month and arrange them in chronological order.

Clock Worksheets

Prepare clock worksheets which consist of a series of clock faces without hands. Print a time beneath each clock face. Have the children draw in the hands on each clock face to indicate the time written below. Have older children fill in numerals on each clock also.

Recording the Sun's Movements

Give each child a posterboard circle. Have the child punch a hole in the center of the circle and push a pencil or stick half way through it. Have the children stick these devices into the ground in a sunny spot. Every hour, children mark the shadow of the pencil on the circle with a colored marker. This primitive sundial will introduce the children to the concept of telling time without a clock.

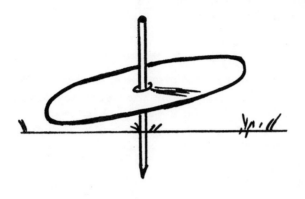

4. Weight

Bathroom Scale

Bring a bathroom scale to the class and have the children weigh themselves with teacher assistance. Keep individual records on each child comparing his or her weight with and without shoes, holding various objects, etc.

Exercise Using Play Dough or Clay

Place two equal sized balls of clay on a balance scale. Take them both off the scale and change the shape of one of the balls into an oblong. Before weighing the clay again, lead the children in a discussion of the possibility of a change in weight in the altered ball.

Weighing Eggs

This experiment must be prepared in advance. Blow out the inside of one egg and hardboil another. Show the children the two eggs, identical in appearance. Have the children discuss the probable weight of the eggs. Weigh the eggs. Have the children guess why the eggs don't weigh the same. Then demonstrate how the eggs were prepared.

Mathematical Balance

Construct or purchase a balance scale. Keep it on a table with several small objects. Have the children weigh each object and record the weights on a piece of paper. Let the children experiment creatively with weighing the objects (for example, weighing two objects at once, etc.)

4. Volume

Jean Piaget's theory of conservation includes teaching the concept of constancy. At some level in their development, children begin to realize that the number of items or quantity of a substance remains constant even though the spatial distribution changes. For example, the teacher pours liquid from a tall skinny jar into a short fat jar. The children observe and are asked, "Is there still as much water in this jar as there was in the first?" The teacher then pours the water back into the first jar. Children observe, discuss and decide.

Measuring Ingredients

Take advantage of occasions other than cooking when children can measure and keep track of ingredients. For example, soapflake paint requires a mixture of soapflakes, water and tempera paint. Measure each ingredient and record the amount used each time it is prepared. An even simpler substance to make is paste. Have the children keep careful records of the amount of water and flour used to obtain the right consistency of paste.

Pints, Quarts and Gallons

Place plastic measuring jars and bottles either near a sink or on the arithmetic table. Children experiment by filling them with either water or sand. Give the children specific tasks to solve, such as how many pints of water it takes to fill the quart bottle.

H. GRAPHS AND CHARTS

Children should be introduced to graphs and charts by means of activities and projects in which their personal involvement is maximized. Tailor topics used to the indigenous interest of the students. Subjects may include the color of hair of students in the room, the kinds of shoes worn by the students, the students' favorite foods, the time they go to bed at night, chores they have to do at home, etc. (See Chapter 7, Social Studies, for illustrations of several such graphs.)

A graph can be a check list, a line graph or building columns. Examples are:

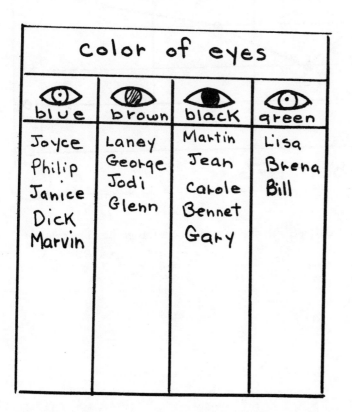

Each child adds his/her name to the proper column.

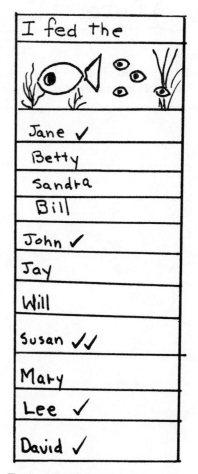

Each child checks his/her name after he/she feeds the fish.

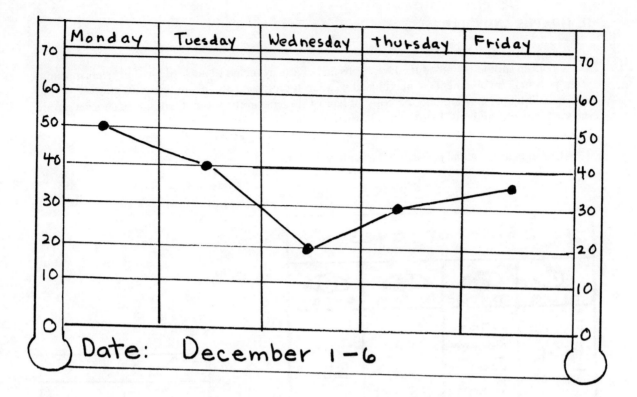

Date: December 1-6

As the child checks the temperature each day, he/she places a mark on the graph. The teacher connects the marks at week's end.

I. MONEY

The study of money teaches children the ability to recognize coins and also teaches them value concepts. The following suggestions are listed in order of increasing difficulty.

Rubbing Coins

Bring or have the children bring genuine coins to school for pencil rubbings. Have the children place a piece of typing paper over a coin and shade the paper over the coin with the side of the pencil lead. Use different denominations.

Play Money

Set up a grocery store or general merchandise shop by using large cardboard cartons and building blocks. The teacher and the children bring empty food cartons, cans, price tags, toy fruits and vegetables, etc., to school. Provide the children with play money to make purchases and let them pretend to shop and purchase food.

Listening for Coin Combinations

This activity was suggested by Heard. Put a nickel inside a small match box. Tell the children that there is five cents inside the box. They must determine if it is one nickel or five pennies. Repeat with other combinations of coins.

Feltboard Piggy Bank

Prepare a feltboard piggy bank with a large center hole (see illustration), and many felt coins. Make the coins by drawing them on posterboard, labeling each coin with its value, and gluing felt on the reverse side. This activity may be played in two ways:
1. The teacher asks the child to place a certain amount of money in the bank; or
2. The teacher puts a certain combination of coins in the bank and asks the child to add up the money in the bank.

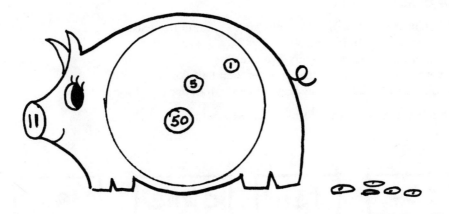

Matching Coins

Prepare a box of pairs of domestic and foreign coins. Have the children match the coins.

Posterboard Prices

Staple eight large pockets to a full sized piece of posterboard. Mark each pocket with a price. If desired, laminate the entire board and slit the pockets to allow an opening. Prepare a number of product cards, each containing a picture of an item and its price. Have the children place each card in the appropriate pocket according to price.

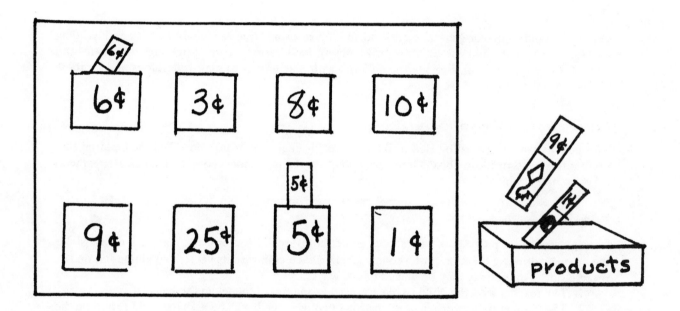

Money Cards for Matching

Prepare and laminate four sets of cards, each set to contain five cards:
1. The symbols: 1, 5, 10, 25, and 50
2. The words: one, five, ten, twenty-five and fifty
3. The words: penny, nickel, dime, quarter, and half dollar
4. An actual penny, nickel, dime, quarter and half dollar taped to the cards.

Have the children match the cards, forming five separate piles.

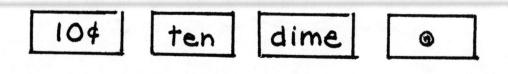

Money Card Equivalents

Glue coins (singly and in combinations) on 6" × 9" cards. Write the equivalent sum beside the coins. Cover the cards with clear contact paper and cut each card down the center in puzzle fashion. Have the children match the pieces.

Worksheets for Primary Grades

Prepare a worksheet by tracing the five coins in the spaces across the top of the page and labeling each with its value. In the far left hand column, list various amounts of money. The children are to place a check under each coin column for each coin in each denomination necessary to make up the sum given on the left.

	50¢	25¢	10¢	5¢	1¢
11¢			✓		✓
23¢			✓✓		✓✓✓
42¢		✓	✓	✓	✓✓

Any combination is acceptable if it is arithmetically correct. Have small groups of children compare their answers to observe different combinations.

J. FRACTIONS

Concrete Operations

Children observe the teacher when she breaks a piece of chalk in half, cuts an apple into fourths, divides the class into thirds, etc. Explain the process of dividing a whole into parts as the activities take place.

Fraction Boxes

Draw four large squares, circles or rectangles in the bottom of empty stocking boxes. Leave one figure whole (label it "1") and divide the remaining three figures into halves, thirds and fourths. Cut out matching shapes from construction paper and cut them up according to the divisions indicated in the drawings in the stocking box. You may wish to color code the sections to make recognition easier. Have the children fit the construction paper pieces into the matching outlines inside the box.

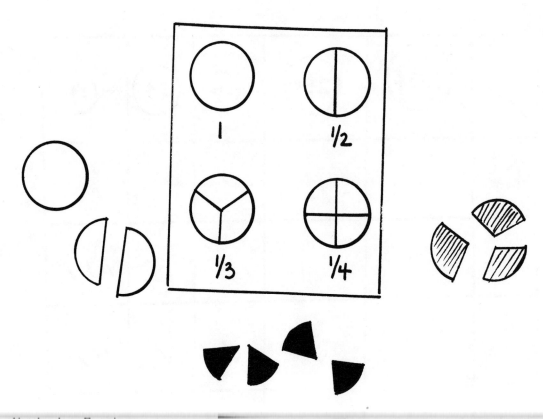

Cutting into Fractions

Give children several like geometric shapes cut out of paper, such as squares, rectangles, triangles or circles. They cut the first shape in half and paste the halves on construction paper. The children then divide the second shape three ways into thirds and the third, four ways into fourths, and paste the pieces on separate sheets of construction paper.

128

K. ADDITION AND SUBTRACTION

Chalkboard Exercises

The teacher draws two blue dots and one red dot on the chalkboard. He/she asks, "How many blue dots have I drawn?" "How many red dots have I drawn?" "How many dots have I drawn altogether?" This exercise may be written as an equation.

$$O \; + \; O \; + \; O \; =$$

This exercise can be done with colored marbles. Give each child a number of marbles in different colors. Have them tell you the number of marbles they have in each color as well as the total number.

Number Line

Tape a number line to the floor. Prepare task cards to accompany the number line. Examples of task cards are:

         Start on 1 and take 2 steps forward.
         Start on 3 and take 1 step backward.
         Start on 7 and take 2 steps forward.

Children may play in pairs or the class may be divided into two groups which play against each other. A player picks a task card and follows its directions. Each time a child lands on a number, he calls its name. If he or she is correct, he or she (or his or her team) makes a point.

Addition Combinations

The teacher prepares nine exercise cards. Label each card with a number from two to ten. List equations under each number for the child to fill in. The equations will be the various combinations of numbers which may be added together to form the number indicated at the top of the card. Give the children round discs with numerals printed on them and have them place the discs in the proper position on each card.

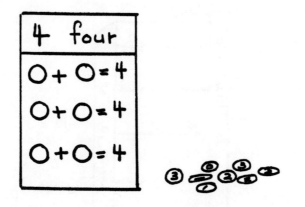

Frame Arithmetic

After the children have learned some basic addition concepts, give them simple lessons using empty frames. Frame lessons are usually a first grade exercise. Examples:

$$6 - 1 = \square$$
$$4 + 1 = \square$$
$$\square - 3 = 2$$
$$2 + 2 = \square$$
$$2 + 1 + 3 = \square$$

Addition-Subtraction Puzzle Cards

With a black marking pen, print simple addition and subtraction problems on one end of 4" × 6" cards and print the answer to each problem on the other end of each card. Cut the cards jigsaw puzzle style and mix up the pieces. Have the children match them.

Number Ladder Game

This is a game that has been used successfully in British Infant Schools to teach addition and subtraction. The game requires one die, two pipe cleaner dolls and a ladder made out of posterboard. Two children play. They begin by placing their dolls at the bottom of the ladder. The children take turns throwing the die and moving their dolls up the ladder according to the number on the die. The first child to reach the top wins. Children can be taught the concept of subtraction by having them start at the top of the ladder and move their dolls downward to throws of the dice.

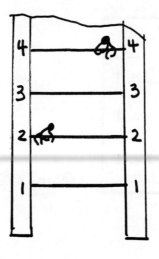

Addition and Subtraction Bingo

Prepare bingo cards containing numbers. Write simple addition and subtraction problems on the chalkboard one by one. If the child's card contains the number which is the answer to the problem, he covers it. The first player who covers all the numbers on his bingo card wins.

Crossword Puzzles with Numbers

Make up a simple "crossword" puzzle with simple addition, subtraction or multiplication problems as the "definitions." Use easy problems to teach the commutative property.

	Across		Down
1.	2 + 2	1.	3 + 1
2.	3 + 3	2.	4 + 2
3.	3 + 4	3.	5 + 2
4.	1 + 10	4.	6 + 5
5.	4 + 8	5.	6 + 6

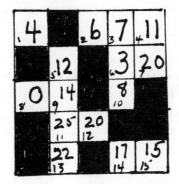

131

L. METRICS

It is important to introduce the language of metrics into the vocabulary of young children. The following table, for teacher reference only, is an easy exposition of the metrical structure. Unit indicators may be applied to liters and grams as well as meters.

kilometer	(km)	1000
hectometer	(hm)	100
decameter	(dkm)	10
meter	(m)	1
decimeter	(dm)	1/10
centimeter	(cm)	1/100
millimeter	(mm)	1/1000

An easy way to introduce children to metrics is through cooking, using the liter measurements on a measuring cup instead of the standard pints and quarts generally used in the United States. In the recipe shown here, the "ml" represents milliliters.

Play Dough

> 500 ml flour
> 125 ml salt
> 175 ml water
> a few drops of food coloring
> a few drops of oil of clove (optional)

> Knead well and store in a tightly covered container.

Centimeter Rods

Using commercial centimeter rods such as Cuisenaire Rods®, teachers can design a number of useful worksheets for young children. In the following example, children match the rods to their silhouettes, color the silhouettes the appropriate color, and record the measurement of each silhouette.

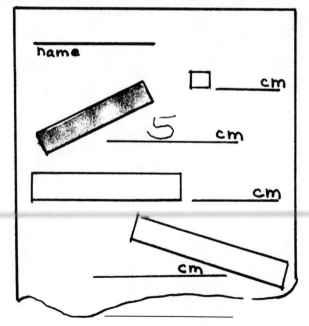

Measuring with Strings

Give each child a length of string, a metric ruler, scissors and a worksheet like the one shown below. Have the children place the string over each line on the worksheet and cut it the same length. The children then remove the string from the worksheet, measure it and record the result on the sheet.

Paper Clip Chains

Have the children make chains by linking paper clips together. Let them measure the chain using a metric stick. If desired, attach the chains to a bulletin board or chart and record the length of each chain next to it.

Finding the Number of Grams

The smallest rod in a set of centimeter rods is a white cube. For all practical purposes, it weighs approximately 1 gram. Provide children with a balance scale and several lightweight objects. Have the children determine the number of grams in each object by adding one centimeter cube at a time to the cup until the scale is balanced. They count the number of cubes used with each object to balance the scale to determine its weight in grams.

Prepare a worksheet picturing the same objects that the children weigh. Have the children record their findings.

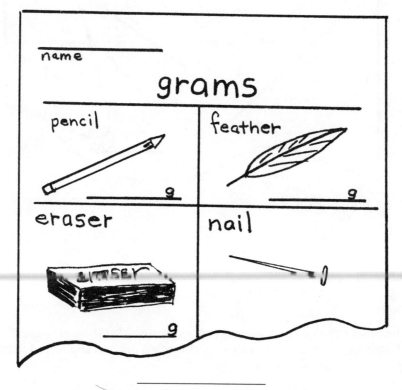

Since music is an integral part of our society, it should be included as an integral part of the early childhood curriculum. The teacher may use a variety of musical experiences such as movement, singing, rhythm band and listening. These activities may be offered independently and informally during the school day or may be combined and planned as a music lesson.

A. MOVEMENT

Movement consists of planned or spontaneous rhythms and informal dance patterns. Through musical expression, youthful energies can be channeled into meaningful experiences. Group activities for young children are very simple, but group activities become sequentially more organized as the child advances into the first, second, and third grades.

Space is essential to an adequate dance program. Large areas promote freedom and exuberance. By rearranging furniture for music, you can increase the space available for a dance program.

Eurhythmics are body movements to improvised music. Eurhythmics include such skills as:

Non-locomotor	*Locomotor*
nodding	walking
clapping	hopping
kicking	jumping
bending	tip-toeing
arm-swinging	skating
swaying	marching
stretching	galloping
twisting	crawling
turning	trotting
	skipping
	whirling and spinning

Rhythms also include locomotor and non-locomotor skills. Rhythms may be used with poems, songs, and dances. Young children are usually introduced to rhythms through nursery rhymes and finger plays. For group action, the following rhythmic words are suggested:

giants	bees
fairies	butterflies
astronauts	mice
clowns	rabbits
monsters	lions
airplanes	alligators
trains	ducks
see-saws	elephants
windmills	horses
elves	frogs
	kangaroos
	pigs
	kittens
	puppies
	gorillas
	dinosaurs

Props that accompany rhythmic words are scarves, balloons, bells, balls, drums, tom-toms, and other percussion instruments.

1. Rhythmic Word Pictures

Rhythmic words can be expanded into rhythmic word pictures. The following suggestions are simple stories that may be accompanied by appropriate piano music or a rythmic drum beat. The teacher describes the scenario and the children act it out, while listening for cues from the piano.

1. Children pretend they are flowers opening in the sun. Rain comes softly, then harder, and the flowers close.

2. Children pretend to be giants walking through the forest. They shake the earth and knock down some trees.

3. Witch's Brew:

Children sit in a circle around a large cooking pot. They take turns pretending to throw odious ingredients into the pot, announcing each addition out loud: spider eggs, frog tongues, snake tails, etc.

After everyone has participated, the children stir the brew with imaginary spoons; then they "eat" it and turn into witches. Now all join in a witch dance with musical accompaniment. (If desired, have the children prepare witch hats out of construction paper in advance to wear during the dance.)

4. Falling Snowflakes: Half the class pretends to be asleep; the other half are snowflakes. The snowflakes chant:
We are little snowflakes floating to the ground.
Shhh, shhh, we don't make a sound.
The children are asleep but when they open their eyes,
The beautiful white snow will be a big surprise.

Unknown

138

5. One child is the mother cat. The rest of the children hide under tables, in closets, etc. The mother searches for her kittens and each time she finds one, she leads it home.

6. Half of the children are bees; the other half flowers. The bees buzz around the room gathering honey from the flowers. The children then reverse roles.

7. The children are frogs in a pond, leaping from lily pad to lily pad. Rain begins to fall and they hide under rocks (the tables or other furniture).

8. Children are kernels of corn sitting in a frying pan. The pan heats up and soon the corn begins to pop.

9. Children are autumn leaves falling from the trees. As the wind blows, more and more leaves fall and swirl to the ground.

2. Finger Plays and Rhythmic Poems

Another means of initiating children into a metric beat and introducing them to patterns of cadence is through the use of finger plays and rhythmic poems. Usually, the teacher acts as a conductor and leads the exercises.

1. Jack in the Box

(Children squat)
Teacher: Jack in the box, Jack in the box
All shut up tight.
Jump, Jack, jump!
Out in the bright sunlight. (Children jump up.)

2. Open them, shut them

Open them, (open hands) shut them (close hands)
Give a litle clap.
Open them, shut them
Give a little clap
Open them, shut them
Fold them in your lap.

Creep them, creep them
Right up to your chin
Creep them, creep them,
Right up to your chin,
Open wide your little mouth
But do not let them in.

Unknown

139

3. Two little apples

Way up in the apple tree (arms over head)
Two little apples smiled at me. (hold up two fingers)
I shook that tree as hard as I could,
Down came the apples,
Mmmm were they good! (pat stomach)

Unknown

4. Ten Little Soldiers

Ten little soldiers standing in a row, (fingers straight up)
They all bow down to the captain so. (fingers bend)
They march to the left.
They march to the right.
They stand up straight ready to fight.
Along comes a man with a great big gun—
Bang, bang, bang, see them all run.

Unknown

5. (Fifteen) Little Indians (Fill in the number equal to the number of children in the room)

Fifteen little Indians, on a nice fall day
Jumped on their ponies and rode far away
They galloped in the meadow and they galloped up a hill
They galloped so fast that they all took a spill.

Unknown

6. Taking a Walk

Taking a walk was so much fun
We didn't hurry; we didn't run
We watched for birds; we watched for bees.
We looked at all the lovely trees.

Unknown

7. Touching

I'll touch my hair, my lips, my eyes.
I'll sit up straight and then I'll rise.
I'll touch my ears, my nose, my chin
Then I'll quietly sit down again.

Unknown

8. Friends

I have two friends (hold up 2 fingers)
And they have me (hold up 1 more finger)
Two friends and me make 1, 2, 3.

Unknown

9. Two Lonely Children
   (Place thumbs inside fists)

One day, a little girl came out of her house. (one thumb pops out of a fist)
She looked up the street, (thumb points to ceiling)
She didn't see anybody.
She looked down the street, (thumb points to floor)
She didn't see anybody.
She looked across the street, (thumb points horizontally)
She didn't see anybody.
She was very lonely, so she went back in her house. (thumb returns to fist)

One day, a little boy came out of his house. (the other thumb pops out of fist)
He looked up the street, (repeat movements of first verse)
He didn't see anybody.
He looked down the street,
He didn't see anybody.
He looked across the street,
He didn't see anybody.
He was very lonely, so he went back in his house.

One day, both children came out of their houses. (both thumbs pop out of fists)
They looked up the street. (both thumbs point to ceiling)
They didn't see anybody.
They looked down the street, (both thumbs point to floor)
They didn't see anybody.
They looked across the street (thumbs point horizontally to each other)
They saw each other.
They walked across the street, shook hands, (hook thumbs)
And they weren't lonely again.

                    Unknown
         _____

141

3. Rhythmic Songs

The following chant comes from a Headstart program in Atlanta, Georgia. It is lively and the children enjoy it.

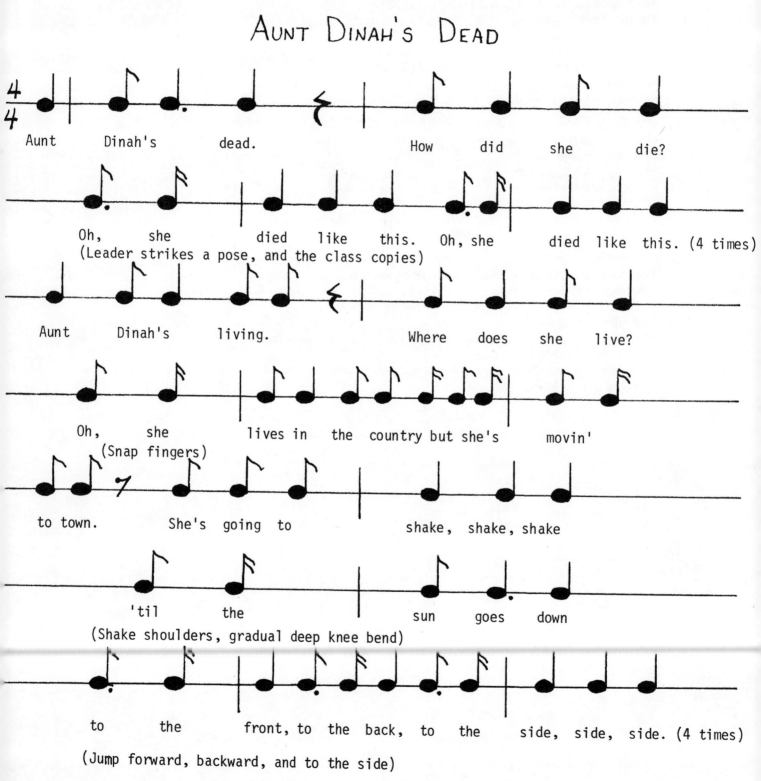

AUNT DINAH'S DEAD

Aunt Dinah's dead. How did she die?

Oh, she died like this. Oh, she died like this. (4 times)
(Leader strikes a pose, and the class copies)

Aunt Dinah's living. Where does she live?

Oh, she lives in the country but she's movin'
(Snap fingers)

to town. She's going to shake, shake, shake

'til the sun goes down
(Shake shoulders, gradual deep knee bend)

to the front, to the back, to the side, side, side. (4 times)

(Jump forward, backward, and to the side)

142

FIVE LITTLE DUCKS

UNKNOWN

Five little ducks went out to play, o-ver the hill and far a-way,

Moth-er duck said quack, quack, quack and four lit-tle ducks came waddling back.

Five Little Ducks

Five little ducks went out to play (hold up 5 fingers)
Over the hill and far away. (hands wave up and down for hills)
Mother duck said, "Quack, quack, quack." (softly)
And four little ducks came waddling back.

Four little ducks went out to play.
Over the hill and far away.
Mother duck said, "Quack, quack, quack."
And three little ducks came waddling back.

Continue the same til "no little ducks."

No little ducks came out to play
Over the hill and far away.
Mother duck said, "QUACK, QUACK, QUACK." (Very LOUD)
And five little ducks came waddling back.

BEND AND STRETCH

UNKNOWN

Bend and stretch   Reach for the stars

Here comes Jup- i- ter there goes Mars   Oh

Bend and stretch   Reach for the sky

Stand on tip toe   oh so high

LIKE A LEAF

Like a leaf or a fea-ther in the win-dy win-dy wea - ther we will

whirl a - round and twirl a - round and all fall down to - ge - ther

Directions:

    Children stand and wave arms above their heads as branches of a tree.
    Turn around one way for whirl and back the other way for twirl.
    Then fall down.

LISTEN TO YOUR FINGERS

Unknown

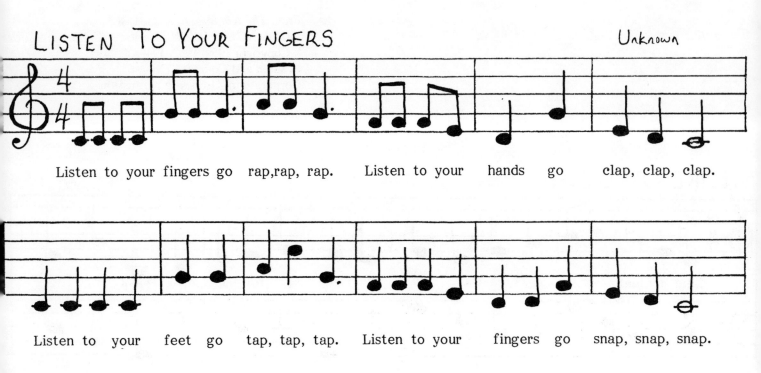

Listen to your fingers go rap, rap, rap.   Listen to your hands go clap, clap, clap.

Listen to your feet go tap, tap, tap.   Listen to your fingers go snap, snap, snap.

Little Red Box
   (sung to the tune of "Polly-Wolly Doodle")

I wish I had a little red box
To put the bad boys (girls) in.

I'd take them out and (clap, clap, clap)
And put them back again.

I wish I had a little red box
To put the good boys in.
I'd take them out and (kiss, kiss, kiss)
And put them back again.

                    Unknown

In a Cottage (sung to the tune of "Hush Little Baby")

In a cottage in the wood (fingers draw an imaginary rectangle)
A little man by the window stood (hold hands in front of eyes as binoculars)
Saw a rabbit hopping by (2 fingers hop horizontally)
Knocking at his door (knock twice)

"Help me, help me, help!" he said, (hands on shoulders then straight up—twice)
Or that hunter will shoot me dead." (point finger as it if were a gun)
"Little rabbit come inside (beckon rabbit)
And safely you will hide." (pat rabbit)

146

Ten Little Indians

Ten children are selected and each is given a number from 1-10. The children stand in a row. As each child's number is sung, that child squats and stays down. The song is then sung backwards and the children stand as their number is called.

1 little
2 little
3 little Indians
4 little
5 little
6 little Indians
7 little
8 little
9 little Indians
10 little Indian braves

The teacher or a student may use a tom-tom or drum to beat out the rhythm of the song.

---

4. Rhythm Games

Indian Tom-Tom Game

Children sit in a circle Indian style. Place tom-tom in the center. Select one child to be "it" and blindfold him or her. The other children chant drum beats and softly slap their upper legs. "It" tries to locate the tom-tom while blindfolded and then beat it.

Echo Rhythm Patterns

The teacher claps out a rhythm pattern and the children repeat it. For variety, switch from clapping to snapping, tapping or slapping the pattern, and have the children do the same.

Name Rhythms

The teacher "taps" name rhythms on a drum. Each child stands when he or she hears the pattern that matches his/her name. Two or more children may stand at a time.

B. DANCING

Dancing encourages free movement to a rhythmic beat. Use a record player, piano, or other instrument to create the rhythm. Encourage creative movements and make sure the child feels free to improvise.

One means of promoting creativity is to allow children to select a rhythm band instrument and then encourage them to devise their own dance sequence by combining movement with playing the instrument. When children devise their own dance sequences, they may vary the timing (fast or slow), the level (high or low from the floor), or the dance pathway. Pathways may follow conventional patterns such as a circle or square, or they may be irregular.

At different points of the pathway the child may strike his or her instrument, leap, turn, squat, etc., creating a dance pattern which he or she can repeat.

When they are played records which have a rhythmic beat, children will often improvise their own dances. Provide children various accessories such as scarves, bells and balloons to enhance creative movement.

The following are popular and successful dance suggestions for use with young children.

Skip To My Lou

folk song

Skip to My Lou

Children stand in a circle.
Two children hold hands and skip around the inside of the circle.
All sing:

    Skip, skip, skip to my Lou.
    Skip, skip, skip to my Lou.
    Skip, skip, skip to my Lou.
    Skip to my Lou, my darling.

One child returns to circle, the other one skips alone.
All sing:

    Lost my partner, what'll I do?
    Lost my partner, what'll I do?
    Lost my partner, what'll I do?
    Skip to my Lou, my darling.

Child taps another child on the shoulder.
All sing:

    Found a partner, skip to my Lou.
    Found a partner, skip to my Lou.
    Found a partner, skip to my Lou.
    Skip to my Lou my darling.

Both children hold hands and skip around the circle.
Repeat first verse.

BLUEBIRD

American Folk Song

Blue bird blue bird through my window Blue bird blue bird through my win - dow

Blue bird blue bird through my window Oh John-ny I am ti - red

Bluebird

Directions:

1. Children stand in a circle.
   All sing, "Bluebird" while one child, the bluebird, walks in and out of the circle.
2. Bluebird stops in front of another child and taps him or her on the shoulder.
   All sing, "Take a little boy (girl) and tap him (her) on the shoulder." Repeat this line 3 times and then sing, "Oh Johnny I am tired."
3. The child tapped is now the bluebird. The first child rejoins the circle.

150

Step and Make a Bow

Have the children choose partners and walk around the room as they sing. Repeat the words four times during the song. Each time the words are sung, the children take three steps, then bow or curtsey to their partner.

Variations include:

1. Slide and slide and slide and make a bow.
2. Hop and hop and hop and hop and make a bow.
3. Skip and skip and skip and make a bow.

C. SINGING

For the child, singing is the outward expression of inward joy. Although it is the basis for an organized music lesson, singing may also be used throughout the day informally. For instance, children may be invited to sing while putting equipment away, while playing, during work period, while cleaning tables, etc. Chants and original tunes spread contagiously through a group of busy students. Using a descending minor third, the natural tones for the very young, the teacher might initiate a chant, "Mary, pick up your toy." Also, familiar tunes such as "The Farmer in the Dell" adapt well to new words. (For example, "We're cleaning up the room, heigh-ho the dairy-oh, we're cleaning up the room.")

Accompany singing with various instruments such as the piano, pitch pipe, resonator bells, tone bells, auto-harp, guitar, ukelele, banjo, drum, and tom-tom, as well as record albums or tapes.

Before starting a song, Montessori teachers usually strike a tone bell so all children will begin on the same note. They recommend that songs range from middle C to high C for young children.

1. Singing Activities

Chant for Names

This chant, used by Bereiter and Engelmann to encourage children to learn each other's names plus initial consonant sounds, is introduced by the teacher who uses any tune:

> The beginning says <u>L</u>
> And the end says isa
> Put them both together and they say Lisa.[1]

Welcome Back Song (for children who have been sick)

Sung to the tune of Frere Jacque

Teacher and class:	"Where is Jodi?"
	"Where is Jodi?"
Jodi:	"Here I am."
	"Here I am."
Teacher:	"How are you today, Miss?" (Sir?)
Jodi:	"Very well, I thank you."
Teacher:	"Glad you're back."
	"Glad you're back."

---

[1]Carl Bereiter, Siegfried Engelman, *Teaching Disadvantaged Children in the Preschool,* © 1966, p. 218. Reprinted by permission of Prentice Hall, Inc., Englewood Cliffs, New Jersey.

Winter Song

The Peabody Language Development Kit[1] uses the old nursery tune of "Farmer in the Dell" to elicit singing responses from individual children. Example:

"What do you wear when it's cold?"
"What do you wear when it's cold?"
"Heigh-ho, it's cold today."
"What do you wear when it's cold?"

Possible answers: "I wear a heavy coat" or "I wear a big warm sweater."

_____

Learning the Scale

Olga Maynard[2] contends that if children can learn the alphabet or nursery rhymes without intensive drilling, they can also learn the musical scale. The following is an example of a simple tune to help children learn the musical scale.

First	I	sing	one	note,	then	it	climbs	up	high,"
c	c	c	c	d	e	e	e	e	f

"Up	and	up	it	goes,	'til	it	hits	the	sky."
g	g	g	g	a	b	b	b	b	c

_____

Melody Lines

In the British Infant Schools, children are shown a copy of the melody line on a staff. As they sing, they observe that the notes go up and down on the page as the pitch goes up and down in a song.

_____

Metronome

In another British Infant School activity the children sing a song three times. For each rendition, the teacher sets a metronome at a different speed, thus introducing the children to the concept of tempo.

_____

2. Songs

Many song books for young children are available and they usually include songs and dramatic plays with accompanying music. The songs shown here are perennial favorites.

_____

[1]*Peabody Language Development Kit,* Level P, American Guidance Service, Inc.
[2]Maynard, Olga *Children and Dance and Music* New York: Charles Scriber's Sons, 1968, p. 121.

May There Always Be[1] . . .

The teacher sings the following song, which was composed by an unknown Russian girl, and then asks the children to suggest other things that they are thankful for. The suggestions might be written on the chalkboard or a chart tablet, then put into the song to make more verses.

Children often suggest such items as flowers, puppies, candy, toys, Christmas, birthday parties, summer, swimming. Each class will contribute something different and since the children composed the words, they will want to sing the song often.

[1]Used by permission of the copyright owner, Lawson-Gould Music Publishers, Inc.

The Lion

"The Lion" can be used the teach the concepts of "soft" and "loud." Beginning with a whisper, the children gradually raise their voices to a roar.

This cumulative song is similar to "Old MacDonald"

I Bought a Rooster

American Folk Song

1. I bought a roost-er, my roost-er pleased me, I fed my roost-er on a green ber-ry tree. My lit-tle roost-er went cock-a-doo-dle doo-dle doo-da-ly doo-da-ly doo-da-ly doo. 2. I bought a cat__, my cat pleased me, I fed my cat on a green ber-ry tree. My lit-tle cat__ went Meow! Meow!

3. I bought a dog__, My lit-tle dog__ went Bow! Wow!

4. I bought a pig__, My lit-tle pig__ went Oink! Oink!

156

Mary Wore a Red Dress

American Folk Song

This is a participation song which teaches color. Change the name, Mary, to a child's in the class and describe, in color, his or her clothes. The child stands as children sing to him or her.

Most children are familiar with "Frere Jacque" but there are many other songs from foreign lands that appeal to young people and that are easy to learn. The following two songs have proved popular in the pre-kindergarten, kindergarten, and primary grades.

UNO, DOS Y TRES   Children's Counting Song   (Cuba)

Uno, dos y tres   quatro, cinco, seis   Siete, o-cho   nueve   y a-hora, diez

la-la la-la la la-la la-la la la-la-la la-la la la la

la-la la-la la la-la la-la la la-la la-la la la.

KINDERGARTEN SONG FROM MEXICO

Gal- li- to roos-ter, Gal- lin- o hen, la- piz pen- cil, plum- a pen

Kindergarten Song From Mexico

Repeat the melody:
  Gallito. . . . . rooster
  Gallina. . . . . hen
  Lapiz. . . . . pencil
  Pluma. . . . . pen
  Ventana. . . . . window
  Puerta. . . . . door
  Techo. . . . . ceiling
  Piso. . . . . floor

Ethel Crowninshield's music was published in 1938, but children still enjoy singing her songs today.

Valentines

Tira Lira Lira

German Folk Song

Ti - ra li - ra li ra, grass so green, Ti - ra li - ra

li ra, hear the stream. Ti - ra li - ra li - ra,

sky so clear, Ti - ra li - ra li - ra, spring is here.

Tira lira lira, grass so green,
Tira lira lira, hear the stream.
Tira lira lira, sky so clear,
Tira lira lira, spring is here.

Tira lira lira, in the spring
Orioles and robins gaily sing.
From the leafy branches you can hear
Tira lira lira ringing clear.

D. USE OF INSTRUMENTS

Rhythm band activities may be part of a music lesson or occur freely and exploratively during the day. These activities may be accompanied by records or the piano.

Organization of a rhythm band depends on the readiness of the group. Very young children adapt to these demands only if they are kept simple.

If instrument are not available, dowel sticks, pie pans and lids, and home-made tom-toms will do.

If possible, have the children attend an orchestral performance. If there is no such opportunity available, invite parents or guests who play instruments to the school to perform.

Rhythm Band Activity I

Have the children sit in a circle. Pass out instruments to the children. Make sure no child has the same instrument as that held by the children on either side of him.

Play a short selection on the piano or record player. Have the children accompany it with their instruments. When the song is over, each child passes his or her instrument to the child to the right so that each one now has a different instrument to play. Repeat until each child has a chance to play every instrument.

Rhythm Band Activity II

Give children instruments. The teacher taps out a rhythmic pattern such as "short, short, long." Children repeat the pattern with their own instruments.

You may use a record to establish the pattern. Usually two patterns to a selection will be sufficient.

Jingle Bells March

Children stand in two concentric circles. The inside circle uses bells. The outside circle uses sticks. Play "Jingle Bells" and have the inner circle march one way while the outer circle marches in the opposite direction. When the song is finished, the children change instruments and positions and repeat.

Old Macdonald Band

Have the children sit in a circle and give them instruments. Keep all sticks together, all bells together, etc. The teacher announces which instrument is to be played. The children sing the following song to the tune of Old MacDonald.

Sticks

    We are members of a band
    Click, click, click, click, click (sticks play)
    And in this band we have some sticks
    Click, click, click, click, click (sticks play)
    With a click, click here and a click, click there
    Here a click, there a click, everywhere a click, click
    We are members of a band
    Click, click, click, click, click (sticks play)

Bells
    Ding, ding

Tambourines
    Shake, shake

Drums
    Rat-tat

Musical Instruments Constructed by the Teacher

Nail Chime

Tie a series of nails, graduated in length beginning with 3" size, at regular intervals in a long string. Hang the nail chime near the music center. Use a nail or triangle beater to play it.

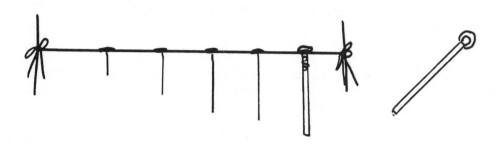

NailoPhone

Drive several long nails into a 2 × 4 (one foot long or longer) at graduated depths, about 1½" to 2" apart. Play the nailophone with a triangle beater.

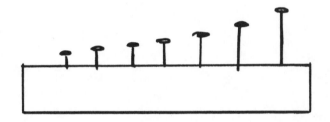

Stringed Instrument

Select a box with a hole in the center (for example, a sturdy empty tissue box). Stretch various sized rubber bands over the opening in the box.

Matching Sounds

The teacher collects 10 or 12 small juice cans, preferably with plastic lids, and covers them with contact paper. Pairs of cans are filled with matching objects, such as thumb tacks, buttons, sand, beans, coins, bells or pieces of chalk. Children match the pairs of cans by the sounds they make when shaken.

Observing Loud and Soft Sounds

Put a handful of rice on a drum and let the child beat the drum with a stick. The rice will move or jump according to how hard the child hits the drum.

Resonator Bells I

Give the child resonator bells and have him or her arrange them from the lowest to the highest pitch.

Resonator Bells II

Give the child three resonator bells: C, D, and E. Ask the child to pick out "Mary Had a Little Lamb." If necessary, help the child by pointing to the first note (E).

Resonator Bells III

Give two children similar resonator bells. One child plays a short musical phrase on the bells. The second child tries to copy the pitch and the rhythm. Reverse roles.

Percussion Play

Children take turns hitting pairs of things together and separating them into "loud" and "soft" piles. Use items such as wood blocks, tennis balls, pillows, books, pot lids, lollipops, and rubber balls.

E. LISTENING TO MUSIC

If young children spend a full day in school some quiet music is appropriate during rest period. You may also wish to use story records that contain songs and orchestral pieces.

At various times you can integrate listening music into your program successfully; for instance, at a child's request or to calm a noisy group.

Painting to Music

Play a soft musical accompaniment on the record player while children paint with cool colors (blues, purples, greens, etc.). The next day, play livelier music while the children paint with warm colors.

———————————

Finding Texture in Music

Ask the children to look around the room and find objects with various textures. Put the objects they name on display and discuss their textures. The teacher also provides different textures in cloth or objects. Play a reording of a musical piece with a variety of moods and melodies, such as "Les Prelude" or "William Tell Overture." As the music progresses, have the children hold up items exhibiting different textures if they think the texture of the item matches the mood of the music.

———————————

Listening for Specific Instruments

Each child traces and cuts out pictures of a violin, a piano, a drum, a trumpet, and a French horn. Play a musical selection which has passages played by these instruments. As each instrument plays, have the child hold up the cut-out of that instrument.

———————————

Listening to Classical Music

In Montessori schools, children enjoy listening to the music of specific composers by means of tape players with ear phones.

———————————

Physical education consists of planned and spontaneous activities that develop fitness and coordination. The developmental level of the child is the determining factor in selecting specific activities. Since large muscle control usually develops before smaller muscles, young children should first be exposed to the freedom of big movement patterns such as running, jumping, and skipping. As the children master basic skills, introduce them to more refined small motor exercises.

Suggestions for activities are divided into two categories: exercises and games. These activities are designed to be used by pre-kindergarten, kindergarten, and primary children.

A. EXERCISES

Exercises include calesthenics, stunts, and tumbling. Each of these areas of the program demand different muscle coordination and balance patterns and thus are a part of the total training. Usually exercises are presented in short sessions, from five to ten minutes long.

1. Calesthenics

Calesthenics or physical fitness movements are basic movement patterns such as locomotor movements, balance patterns, and ball handling movements. Some examples of locomotor movements are:

> crawling
> walking
> running
> climbing
> jumping
> rolling
> hopping
> skipping
> sliding
> galloping

Each of these may be extended to add interest and dimension. For instance:

> walk as a giant walks
> walk as a fairy walks
> walk as a lazy person walks
> walk as if you're going to the dentist
> walk as if you're stepping on sharp stones
> walk as if you're stepping on hot pavement
> walk as if you have a piece of glass in one foot
> walk as if you are very tired
> walk as if your toes hurt

---

2. Balance Patterns

Balance patterns, usually performed in one location, include such movements as:

      standing
      sitting
      twisting
      stretching
      arm swinging

Combine these movements to engage in such routines as:

      bending-stretching
      twisting-turning
      throwing-catching
      jumping-squatting
      pushing-pulling
      jumping-hopping

Balance beam movements might include:

      forward walk
      backward walk
      sideward cross-step
      walk across beam with beanbag on head

Outdoor equipment such as tricycles, bicycles, climbing apparatus, slides, swings, horizontal ladder, jump ropes, wagons, and scooters are all used to promote physical activities. In addition, in some instances children have the use of an obstacle course.

An obstacle course offers challenges in running, climbing, balancing, sliding, and pulling. A qualified instructor should direct the action.

The instructor first explains how each obstacle is to be used and then demonstrates by using it. The class then lines up in a single file and on a starting signal, follows the leader from one obstacle to the next. The entire class should finish in a minimal amount of time, usually no more than 10 minutes.

Example:

Note: If children are mature enough to climb the #1 platform they may do so. Allow only one child at a time on the top of the platform.

3. Ball handling

Free exploration with rubber balls, yarnballs, and beanbags will help children develop ball-handling skills. In addition some guided exercises add interest:

Balls (8", 8½" or 10" balls may be used)
    bounce and catch
    bounce-clap-catch
    toss in the air and catch
    bounce and catch to partner
    kick the ball from a stationary position
    kick the ball from a rolling position
    kick the ball when dropped

Yarnballs
    underhand toss
    dodge ball with two or more players

Beanbags
    toss in the air with one hand, catch with two
    toss, clap and catch with two hands
    toss, turn around, catch
    throw to a partner

4. Stunts

A stunt is an exercise plus imaginative accompanying actions. A stunt may be a simple vignette, a descriptive phrase, or animal imitations. Usually the entire class is involved in stunts at the same time. The following imaginative actions are ideas which teachers can use as models for more elaborate programming:

Elevators
    Child places hands on hips, bends knees slowly into a squat, then rises slowly

See-saw
    Using partners, children hold hands and take turns squatting

Automobiles
    Child places hands on the floor ahead of feet and moves slowly forward, then backward into a parking space

Windmills
    Child stands straight with feet apart, holds arms straight and criss-crosses them in front

Firecrackers
    Child squats down and pops up

Tight Rope Walk
    Child walks a straight line taped on the floor, holding arms straight out to the side

The Ostrich
    Bend body at waist, grasp ankles, keep knees stiff and walk

The Kangaroo
    Feet together, elbows bent, jump.

The Frog
    Hands on hips, deep knee bend, extend one leg to the side, return. Repeat with other leg.

Rooster
    Hold head and chest high. Strut with knees straight and hands at the side of chests. Flap elbows.

Rabbit
    Hands make rabbit ears. Squat and hop.

Bears
    Stiffen legs and touch floor with hands. Slide forward, slowly.

Ducks
    Squat and hold knees with hands. Walk in this position.

Elephants
    Bend forward, hands clasped together. Move them up and down for a trunk and sway from side to side while walking slowly.

Camels
    Bend at waist, grasp lower legs and walk.

Alligators
    Crawl on stomach and make a terrible noise.

Crabs
    Sit, place hands on floor behind body. Raise body off the floor and walk on all fours, backward and forward.

Other Animal Suggestions:
    Roly-poly
    Lame dog run
    Pony Gallop
    Seal walk
    Gorilla Walk
    Lions
    Stork Stand
    Kittens
    Birds
    Fish
    Turtles
    Circus Horse
    Woodpecker tapping

And Even More Suggestions:
    Trucks
    Sailboats
    Airplanes
    Waves
    Log rolls
    Kites
    Skaters
    Swimmers
    Surfboard riders
    Ballet dancers
    Disco dancers
    Firemen
    Organ grinders
    Clowns

    Robots
    Indians
    Lion tamers
    Sleepwalkers
    Back packers
    Mountain climbers

5. Tumbling

Tumbling requires the use of a mat. Movements usually consist of follow-the-leader actions by two or more children. Children may make up their own actions or use variations of the following:

Forward Roll (Somersault): Start in a squatting position with knees apart, hands on mat between knees. Roll forward and over.

Backward Roll: Squat, keep back curved, roll back placing hands on floor behind head. Push with hands and continue to roll until completely flipped over.

Side Roll: Roll sideways from one end of the mat to the other.

6. Trampoline

One teacher should stand at each end of the trampoline for safety. The children may practice high and low jumps, fast and slow jumps. Some specific exercises are:

Jump and stop on command.
Jump and turn around in the air.
Jump predetermined amount of times and stop.
Jump on one foot, then the other.

7. Ladder Climbing

Beginners need constant supervision. Some exercises are:

Up and down.
Slow climb then fast climb.
Start with right foot.
Start with left foot.

Summary

If the teacher wants to keep an evaluation on each child's motor progress, the following check list may be used:

Check List for Motor Skills

Name _____ Date _____

	Yes	No
Walking		
Running		
Jumping		
Hopping—left foot 3 times		
Hopping—right foot 3 times		
Throwing a ball—coordination		
Throwing a ball—accuracy		
Sommersault		
Riding a tricycle		
Climbing stairs (up, no hands)		
Climbing stairs (down, no hands)		
Climbing ladder		
Balancing on left foot, 15 seconds		
Balancing on right foot, 15 seconds		
Balance beam		
Catching a ball		
Skipping		

B. GAMES

Games are more than fun; they are an excellent way to teach concepts. Some of the consequences of playing games are: 1) the child is forced into thinking and making responses; 2) repetition in games reinforce the learning process; and 3) children establish social relationships in an informal manner.

Explain each game clearly and simply before game play begins. During play the teacher should remain available but his or her presence should not be intrusive.

1. Pantomine Games

Pantomime games are in fact dramatic play in game form. One child performs a simple action while the others try to guess what he/she is doing. Children may act out their own ideas or use suggestions from the teacher. Possible suggestions are:

jumping rope
riding a bicycle
driving a car
setting the table
chewing gum
saying prayers
going to sleep
eating a lollipop
eating spaghetti
falling down
buttoning a coat
tying a shoe
combing hair
patting a dog
ironing clothes
climbing a ladder
picking flowers
chopping wood
hoing the garden
rowing a boat
jack-in-the-box
flying an airplane
digging a hole
reading a book
breaking a glass
painting the house
sweeping
swimming
crying
shaving
cracking open an egg
cooking
sewing
skipping rope

I fan myself
slapping a mosquito
I'm a ballerina
playing baseball, tennis, golf, football, etc.
moods such as: sadness, happiness, fear, anger, sleepiness
tree blowing in the wind
a young colt first learning to stand up
flowers opening to the sun
bees visiting the flowers
candy melting in the sun
moths fluttering around a candle
a puppy playing with a cat

2. Get Acquainted Games

How do you do?

Teacher says, "I like to say good morning.
          I like to say hello.
          I like to shake the hand
          Of the one I know.
          Hello, (child's name)."

The teacher shakes Mary's hand. Teacher then helps Mary say the poem to another child who repeats it to the next child, etc.

_____

Spin the Bottle

Children sit in a circle. The teacher spins the bottle. When the bottle stops and points to a child, that child says, "My name is _____." The child then spins the bottle.

_____

Remembering Names

Children sit in a circle. One child rolls a ball or tosses a bean bag to another child, calling his or her name as he or she rolls. "I roll the ball to _____."

_____

Call Ball

Children stand in a circle. One player ("it") stands in the center of the circle. He tosses a volleyball into the air and calls another child's name. The child whose name has been called tries to catch the ball after one bounce. If he succeeds, he is then "it" and will toss the ball and call out another child's name. If he misses, the first player continues to call other names until someone catches the ball.

_____

3. Visual Discrimination Games

Removing Colors

Children sit in a circle. Place different colored blocks or strips of paper in the middle of the circle. One child turns around and the teacher removes a block. The child looks and tries to remember which colored block or strip is missing.

_____

I Spy

Teacher begins the game as "it" by saying, "I spy something blue." Children take turns guessing what it is. The child who guesses is then "it."

Policeman, Find My Child!

Teacher is the "mother." She chooses a child to be the policeman. She describes her child, the color of his/her hair, eyes, clothes, etc. Policeman walks around the circle of children and tries to identify the child. When the policeman identifies the correct child, that child becomes the policeman.

Flash Pictures

The teacher flashes a picture containing several shapes. Children take turns trying to recite all of the objects shown on the card. As an alternative, the teacher might draw the objects on the chalkboard and then erase them. As a further alternative, children may draw what they saw on paper rather than listing the objects verbally.

Matching Shapes

Cut out pairs of triangles, circles, squares, etc., from colored construction paper. Hide one set around the room. Put the other set in a basket on the teacher's desk. Have the children search the room. When a child finds a shape, he takes it to the basket, matches it with its mate, and identifies the shape.

Coloring Relay

Outline two identical pictures with a felt marker and tack them to a bulletin board. Divide the children into two teams. Have the teams line up. Give each player a different colored crayon. At the "Go" signal, the first player of each team runs to the picture and colors one clearly defined section, such as an arm, leg, or hat. When finished, he runs back to his team and touches the next player. The next player then colors a section of the picture. The first team to color the whole picture wins.

Alphabet Pictures

Give each child a piece of construction paper with a large letter on it. One idea is to give each child the first letter in the child's name. Have the child draw a picture around the letter. When the pictures are finished, the teacher holds them up in front of the class and the children try to guess what the picture is and what letter was used.

Spy the Object

The teacher selects a small object (i.e. a crayon, chalk, color cube, pencil or other) and shows it to the students. Designate a large area on the floor as home base. The children hide their eyes and the teacher places the object somewhere in the room in plain sight. Then have the children open their eyes and search for the object. As each child spies the object he or she quietly sits down in the home base without telling anyone else where it is.

The others search until all the children have found the object. When all the children are seated, the first one who sat down tells where the object is. Everyone who saw it is a winner.

---

4. Auditory Discrimination Games

Boilerburst

The children stand in a circle with one person ("it") in the center. "It" tells a story on any subject. In the course of telling the story, the child says the word, "Boilerburst." When the rest of the children hear that word they all run away and the storyteller must catch one of them. The person who is caught then becomes "it" and the game starts over again.

Stream of Directions

The children sit in a circle and the teacher gives one child three or four simple tasks to do in sequence. For example, "Go to the desk, get a piece of chalk, draw a circle on the chalkboard, then sit down." After the child performs the requested tasks, the children decide if he or she followed the teacher's directions in proper order.

Who is Humming?

Choose one child who leaves the room. Select another child to be the hummer. All the children rest their heads on their desks. The first player returns and tried to guess who is humming. He or she walks around the room searching. The hummer may stop when the child approaches. When the hummer is caught, he or she is the next one to leave the room.

Statues

Teacher plays the piano or a record. Children run, skip, or dance around the room. When the music stops, they must freeze in their last position. If they move, they are out of the game. The last one remaining is the winner.

———————

Musical Chairs

Set up a number of chairs, equal to the number of children playing minus one, in two rows back to back in the center of the room. Teacher plays the piano or a record. Children walk around the chairs while the music plays; when it stops, they sit. The child left standing is out of the game and one chair is removed from the rows. The last child to remain in the game is the winner.

———————

Skip and Stoop

Children skip around the room to music. When the music stops, they stoop. The last one to stoop each time is out of the game.

———————

Singing Game

Children hide their eyes. Teacher touches one child on the shoulder and asks him/her to sing. After he or she is finished, children open their eyes and try to guess who sang.

———————

Ten Little Indians

Choose ten children. Give each child a number from 1 to 10. The children sing "Ten Little Indians." As his or her number is called, each child stoops. The group then sings the song backwards and each child stands up.

———————

Ring the Bell

Blindfold one child. Another one quietly carries a bell to a corner of the room and rings it. The blindfolded child points in the direction of the bell.

———————

5. Muscular Development Games

Chair Skip

Put enough chairs to seat all the children in a circle. Children stand behind the chairs. Choose one child to be "it." "It" skips around the inside of the circle to music. When the music stops, he or she sits in the nearest chair. The child who is standing behind that chair enters the circle and skips to the music. When all the children are seated, the game may continue in reverse. Children skip around the outside of the circle and stop behind a chair when the music stops. When all are standing, the game ends.

———————

Pass the Ball

Children sit in a circle and pass a large ball around. As each child passes it to his or her neighbor, the children sing:

    You pass the ball around
    It goes from town to town
    And when the little bally stops
    You are out.

The child who has the ball when the word "out" is sung has to drop out of the circle. The circle gets smaller and smaller until there is only one child remaining and that child is the winner.

You pass the ball around   It goes from town to town   And when the little bally stops   You are out!

Relay Races

Divide children into two teams. The teams form two lines. The first child in each line runs (or walks, skips, hops, jumps, etc.) to a specified point and back to the team, touching the next player. This player then repeats the performance until the entire line of children has participated. The team who finishes first wins.

Balance Relay Races

The children run a relay race balancing a beanbag or eraser on their heads.

Tricycle Relay

Divide the children into three or four teams. The teams line up. The first in each line rides a tricycle to a designated spot, returns to the line of children, and touches the next child. The second child then mounts the tricycle and does the same. The team who finishes first wins.

Stop on a Square

Tape several large squares on the floor. Children run from square to square. When the teacher blows a whistle, everyone must stop running. Those not standing in a square are out of the game. The last child in the game wins.

Follow the Leader Train

Children construct a train station with large building blocks. Select one child to be the conductor and another child to be the engineer. Give the rest of the children paper tickets to enter the station. Then the conductor punches a hole in each ticket with a hole puncher. After all are inside the station, the engineer collects the tickets one by one. As a child's ticket is taken, he or she stands in line behind the engineer. When all are ready, the engineer leads them on a trip around the school.

Simon Says

The leader (the teacher or a child) is Simon. Facing the children, Simon gives them a command. The children are to obey all commands which begin "Simon says" but not the commands which do not begin with "Simon says." Any child who obeys a command which does not begin with "Simon says" is out of the game. For very young children, do not omit the phrase, "Simon says."

Touch Tag

One child is "it." The other children run around and "it" tries to tag one of them. If the child is tagged on the arm, then that child must hold his or her arm with the other hand and is now "it."

Duck, Duck, Goose

(Similar to Drop the Handkerchief)
Children sin in a circle. "It" walks around the outside of the circle and says "duck" as he touches each child on the head. He touches one child and says, "Goose." That child must chase "it" around the circle before "it" can get back to "goose's" place. If "it" is caught he must sit in the center of the circle. If "it" makes it back to "goose's" place and sits down before "goose" taps him, "goose" becomes "it."

Roll the Ball (Bowling)

Teacher stands blocks on top of each other on the floor. From a specified point, one child rolls a large ball on the floor toward the blocks and tries to knock them down.

180

Snowmen

Children stand around the room. They are snowmen. One child is the sun and he or she walks around the room, touching each snowman. As he/she touches the children, they begin to melt.

Beanbags

Children take turns throwing beanbags into a box. They keep score on the chalkboard.

---

6. Blindfold or Hide-Your-Eyes Games

Secret Bag

Teacher places different textured articles (such as cotton balls, velvet, straw, crayons, marbles, yarn, buttons, and sandpaper) in a paper bag. Children try to identify objects by feeling and not looking.

Variation: Use solid geometrical shapes for the children to identify, such as cubes, spheres, cylinders, and pyramids.

Muffin Man

One child is blindfolded and sits in the center of a circle. All walk around and sing, "Do you know the muffin man?" When the song ends, the teacher points to one child to be the muffin man. He walks to "it," who tried to identify him by feeling his face.

Identify the Smell

One child is blindfolded and sits in a chair while the others observe. The teacher holds one object at a time close to his nose and he tries to identify the object by its aroma. Use strong smelling articles such as an onion, soap, perfume, spices, vinegar, ammonia, and cabbage.

Who is Tapping?

One child sits in the center of the circle, hiding his/her face. The teacher points to another child in the circle who taps his/her shoe three times. "It" then open his/her eyes and tries to identify the tapper in three guesses.

Dog and the Bone

"It" sits in a chair in the center of the circle and hides his/her eyes. Place an eraser under "it's" chair. The teacher points to one child in the circle who tip-toes quietly to the chair and steals the eraser, returning to his place and hiding it behind him. They all say, "Wake up, doggie, someone stole your bone." "It" then tries to identify the thief in three guesses.

Objects on a Table

Place four or five objects on a table for the children to see. Have them hide their eyes and then remove one object. Children raise their hands if they know which object is missing. After a short period of time call on one of the children to name the missing object. Use more objects with older children.

Who Has Gone From the Room?

All children close their eyes. The teacher taps one child, who leaves the room. Children then open their eyes and raise their hands to state who has left the room.

Variation: One child closes his/her eyes and the teacher chooses someone else to leave the room. The first child then tries to guess who is missing.

Who Am I? or What Am I?

One child is chosen to be "it." "It" leaves the room and the teacher tells the other children to pretend to be an animal (a bunny, a bird, a kangaroo, etc.). The children then imitate that animal. Call "it" back into the room. "It" tries to guess what animal the children are imitating. You can also play the game with adjectives rather than animals. Tell the children to pretend to be hot, cold, sad, angry, etc.

Cat and Mice

Select one child to be the cat. All the other children are mice. The cat pretends to sleep and hides its eyes. The teacher says, "The cat is asleep and all the mice can now have their fun." The mice then find hiding places in the room. When they are all hidden, the teacher wakes the cat up and asks it to find those naughty mice. The cat hunts for the mice and as each mouse is found, he or she returns to his/her seat. The last mouse found is the winner and becomes the next cat.

C. OUTDOOR ACTIVITIES

Time spent outdoors is usually free time for the child. It can be spent on stationary equipment such as jungle gyms or other free form climbing apparatus, swings, slides, large concrete pipes, tetherball posts, and/or a sandpile. Auxiliary furnishings may include tricycles, bicycles, wagons, scooters, balls, beanbags, long jump ropes, hoolahoops, hobby horses, and sand toys.

Hopscotch and Bean Bag Toss

Hopscotch games and a bean bag line and square may be chalked or painted on the pavement. For indoor use, make a design on the floor with masking tape. Very young children should be allowed to play without penalties for stepping on lines.

American Hopscotch

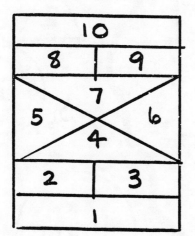

French Hopscotch

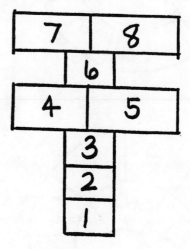

183

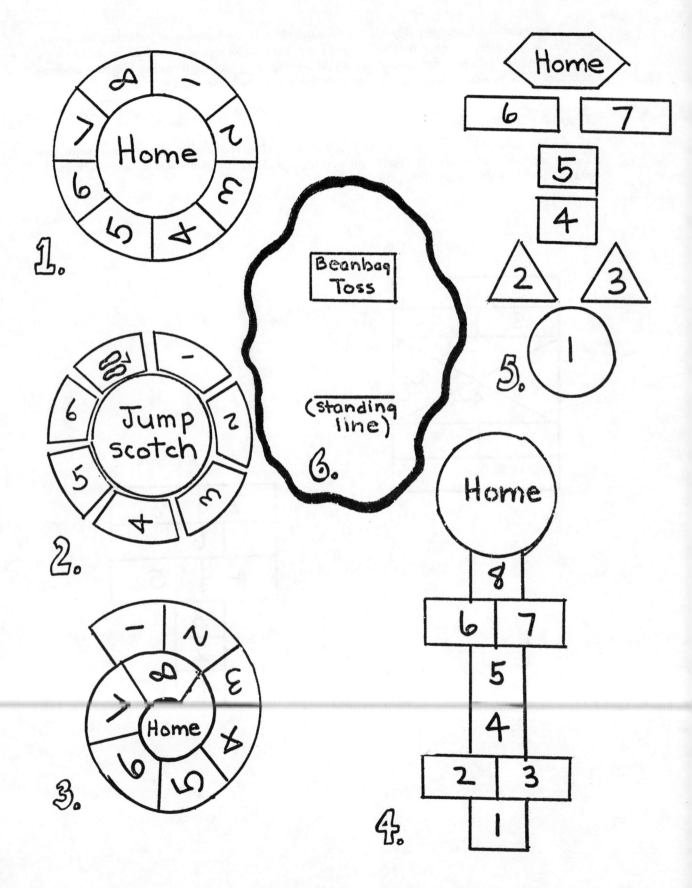

Squirrels and Nut

All the children stand in a circle with their hands cupped behind them. One child ("it") is selected to walk or skip around the outside of the circle and drop a nut or stone into a child's cupped hands. That child then chases "it" around the circle. "It" must try to run back to the chaser's empty space before being tagged. If he does so he joins the circle. If tagged, then "it" must stand in the center of the circle. The chaser now becomes "it" and the game starts all over again.

Skip Tag

All the children skip around except one ("it"). As long as the children are skipping they are safe. "It" tries to tap a child while he or she is not skipping. A child who "it" taps while he or she is not skipping is out of the game.

Stoop Tag

All the children run around except one child who is "it." As long as children are stooping they are safe. "It" tries to touch someone not stooping. If "it" is successful, the child he/she touches is the next "it."

Shadow Tag

This game must be played on a bright, sunny day. One child ("it") chases the others. If "it" can step on another child's shadow, then that child becomes "it."

Red Light

All the children stand behind a starting line except one who stands about twenty feet away facing the others. This child hides his or her eyes and counts to ten. Then, opening his/her eyes, the leader says, "Red light!" Anyone the leader sees moving after the words "Red light!" must return to the starting line. The first child to reach the leader takes his or her place, and the game starts over again. The old leader joins the other children at the starting line.

Statues

All dance or run around until a whistle is blown. Anyone moving after the whistle is blown is out.

Come Along

Select one child to be "it." The other children stand in a circle and "it" walks around the outside of the circle tagging several players and saying, "Come along!" The tagged children follow him and he leads them away from the circle. When they are far away, he shouts, "Home!" All the children run back to their places. The first one "home" is the next "It."

Squirrel in the Tree

Players stand in groups of three. Two children form a "tree" by facing each other and holding hands. The third player, the squirrel, stands between them. One squirrel does not have a "tree" and that squirrel is "it." The leader rings a bell or blows a whistle and all the squirrels must change trees. The squirrel left out becomes "it" for the next game.

Old Witch, What Time Is It?

The teacher or one of the children is the witch. The witch slowly walks around the playground followed by the class. The children ask: "Old witch, what time is it?" The witch answers with a time ("It is one o'clock." "It is three o'clock," etc.) The children keep asking until the witch says, "It is twelve o'clock!" On that cue, the children all run away and the witch chases them. Whomever the witch catches become the next witch.

The teacher may plan science lessons in advance or allow them to develop spontaneously from the expressed interests of the children. The methodology used should emphasize and encourage student participation and exerimentation while minimizing the use of teacher explanations.

It is preferable to teach young children concepts rather than facts. A concept is an interpretation of a situation or idea. A fact is a proven statement. For example, it is a fact that water freezes at 32°F. It is a concept that during the winter, small ponds or lakes freeze over when it gets very cold. Because children are capable of assimilating information within the context of their own experiences, a teacher's task is to broaden their experiences by teaching them concepts in terms of their environment.

Science activities include experiments and demonstrations plus the use of equipment on the science table. Science tables are valuable learning centers as long as the material on them is changed frequently.

The following science activities are divided into four categories:

A. Living Things
B. The Earth
C. Forces, Matter, and Energy
D. The Universe

A. LIVING THINGS

The study of living things includes the study of people, animals, and plants.

1. People

a. The Five Senses

i. Sight

Face Pictures

Cut out pictures of eyes from magazines and paste a pair on each sheet of manila paper (or draw a pair of eyes on each sheet). Give each child a sheet of manila paper containing a pair of eyes and have the children draw faces around the eyes.

Activity to Discover Sources of Light

During a general discussion period, the teacher asks children to suggest where we might find light. The teacher draws the children's answers on a chart tablet. If the children are not responsive, give them hints. Suggested answers are: the sun, moon, stars, electric lights, fire, fireflies, stars, and candles.

Demonstration: Light Rays Can Bend

The teacher puts a pencil in a transparent glass half-filled with water. Children observe that the pencil seems to bend. Put the glass and pencil on the science table for free examination.

Demonstration: Mixing Colors I

Mount colored cellophane on 5" × 5" posterboard frames. Put the cellophane frames on the science table and let the children experiment with looking through one, two or three of them at a time to see how colors mix.

Demonstration: Mixing Colors II

Cover the lights of three flashlights with red, blue and yellow cellophane. Darken the room and by shining the lights independently and then one over the other, demonstrate the mixing properties of colored lights to the children.

Color Wheel

Show the class a color wheel with the three primary colors painted in. Then, as the children observe, mix orange, purple and green paint (using the primary colors) and paint in the orange, purple and green sections of the color wheel. Tack the finished color wheel on the bulletin board. Give the children small color wheels to paint and take home.

Prism and Rainbows

The teacher explains and demonstrates how to use a prism. Children try to be the first to discover the rainbow. Have the children observe the colors carefully and then give them paper and paints (or crayons) so they may create their own rainbows on paper.

Activity Which Emphasizes the Importance of Color

Have the children draw two identical pictures. At one table, the children paint one of their pictures with black and white paint. At a second table they have a choice of many colors to use to paint the second picture. When finished, each child compares the two pictures.

Demonstration of Color Changes

Cut out the body of a peacock from construction paper and tack it to a bulletin board. Give the children manila construction paper feathers to paint. Have them tack their feathers on the bulletin board after they are painted. Prepare three pairs of "eyeglasses" out of cardboard and three different colors of cellophane. Tack the glasses to the bulletin board. Encourage the children to experiment with the glasses and observe color changes in the peacock when it is viewed through different colored glasses.

Tracing Shapes

Give the children parquetry blocks to trace with pencils. They then color the penciled shapes the same color as the corresponding blocks.

An Observation Walk

Label several boxes with words descriptive of leaves in the fall: "round," "pointed," "green," "brown," "red," "yellow," etc. Put the boxes on the science table. Take the children on an observation walk in the fall to look for different kinds of leaves. Have the children bring the leaves back to the classroom and place them in the labelled boxes on the science table.

---

ii. Sound

Sound Travels

The teacher ties a string to a spoon. Children take turns holding the end of the string to their ear while they hit the spoon with a pencil or another spoon. The sound travels up the string and sounds like a bell.

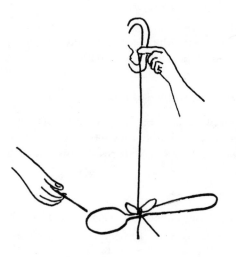

Making Tin Can Telephones

Remove the tops from two empty tin cans. Punch holes in the bottoms of the cans. Connect the cans by at least twelve feet of wire by inserting each end of the wire into the hole in one of the cans and securing it with a button. Give the telephone to two children and have them stand far enough apart so that the wire is stretched taut between them. The children take turns speaking into one can and listening into the other.

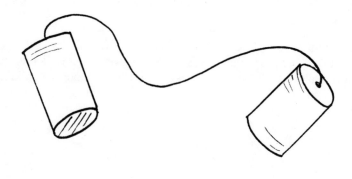

Matching Sounds

Gather together pairs of identical opaque containers with lids (for example, empty film cans or Band-Aid boxes). Put buttons in two containers, rice in two, bells in two, nails in two, sand in two, etc. Have the children match the boxes by shaking them and placing the pairs of boxes giving off identical sounds together.

Guess the Sound

Show the children several objects such as a ball, ruler, marbles, chalk, eraser, pencil, and knife. Have the children hide their eyes and drop one object. The children try to guess what was dropped. Repeat with other objects.

Ball Bouncing

Children hide their eyes and one child bounces a ball several times. Whoever counts the number of bounces correctly is the next ball bouncer.

Listening

Children cover their eyes and remain silent while listening to sounds in the classroom. Then they discuss what they heard.

Listening Walk

Take the children for a listening walk. If possible, take a tape recorder along and record the sounds heard. Back in the classroom, play the tape back and have the children guess what they are hearing.

Taping Play Period

Unknown to the children, the teacher tapes their voices on a recorder while they are playing or working. Play the tape back to them later in the day. Have the children try to identify all the voices they hear on the tape.

Musical Glasses

Fill seven drinking glasses with progressively larger amounts of water. Keep them on the science table in order from the one holding the least amount of water to the one holding the most water. Let the children "play" the glasses with a metal spoon. If bells are available, they may be used to accompany the glasses.

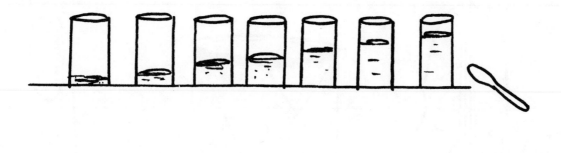

Musical Board

Drive two large nails into the opposite ends of a two-foot board. Stretch a heavy rubber band across them. Let the children pluck the rubber band. Use tighter or looser rubber bands to vary the sound.

Sound Travels

Children experiment by ringing a bell behind a closed door, inside a box, under water, wrapped in cloth, etc. If desired, make a list and record increases and decreases in volume.

Musical Boxes

Place various sized open cardboard boxes on the science table. Stretch one or two rubber bands around each box. Let the children experiment with them.

The Orchestra

Using patterns, each child traces and cuts out three musical instruments. One must be a stringed instrument, one a percussion, and one a wind instrument. The teacher plays a classical record. Children listen to the music. When violins play, the children hold up their string cut outs. When trumpets play, the children hold up their wind cut outs, etc.

---

iii. Touch

Class Discussion

Ask children to describe sensations and textures they can feel. Suggested responses: hot, cold, pressure, pain, sticky, smooth, prickly, rough, soft, hard.

Touch Bulletin Board

Almost any bulletin board that contains a variety of illustrations may be turned into a touch bulletin board. Create "touch" areas out of materials such as sandpaper, satin, velvet, cellophane, burlap, corrugated paper and cotton, and paste them onto parts of the bulletin board figures. Encourage the children to compare the textures of the different areas.

— flower centers are different textures

A Texture Walk

Mark off a "rough" and a "smooth" section on the science table. Each child paints a small box. Take all the children for a walk outdoors with their boxes. Tell half the class to collect smooth articles. Tell the other half to collect rough items. Back in the classroom, the children place their boxes in "rough" or "smooth" sections of the science table.

A Touch Me Box

Place a variety of objects with different textures in a box on the science table. Children take turns trying to identify the objects by touch, either with their eyes closed or blindfolded.

touch me

Sandpaper "Feelies"

These sandpaper "feelies" are fashioned after Montessori sensorial material. Purchase extra fine to coarse sandpaper at a hardware store and mount a piece of each sandpaper on small wooden slabs. Make pairs of each sample so that children may match them as well as comparing the sandpaper boards or arranging them in sequence according to roughness.

Some Montessori boards have five strips of graded sandpaper spaced on a smooth board. A child might use a blindfold while working with this kind of sandpaper board and, while stroking his/her fingers across it, say "rough" or "smooth" with each touch sensation.

Montessori Thermal Containers

Montessori containers are steel cylinders but any screw-type glass or plastic bottle will work as well. Fill two bottles with hot water, two with warm and two with cold. Children separate and match them.

Texture Hunt

Have the children sit in a circle. Let them take turns feeling an object with a noticeable texture (for example, rough). Then have the children walk around the room and find an object with a similar texture. They bring the objects back to the circle and sit down. One at a time, each child displays his/her object and the others decide if it matches. Repeat the hunt with a different texture.

Things That Must be Kept Cold

Draw a large refrigerator (with a freezer) on a bulletin board. Give the children magazines and tell them to cut out pictures of food. Tape pictures of food that must be kept cold on to the refrigerator. Tape pictures of food that needs to be kept frozen on to the freezer.

Comparing Liquids

Fill several plastic boxes half way with a variety of liquids such as vegetable oil, catsup, water, milk of magnesia, milk, soda pop. Let the children experiment with the liquids and discover that liquids have texture also.

Feely Boxes for the Science Table

Instead of using just one "touch me" box, use several shoe boxes with lids as "feely" boxes. Cut a hole in one end of each box. Place different objects in each box, such as a balloon filled with water, ping pong balls, a toy car, sponge balls, or nails. Have the children reach their hands inside each box and guess the contents.

---

iv. Smell

Class Discussion

The teacher brings several items to class for smelling such as dirt, lemon, spoiled potato, medicine, paint, perfume, onion, and candy. Children take turns smelling the items and describing what they smell. Occasionally have a child hold his nose while trying to smell something. What happens?

Guess the Smell

Place a box containing many jars of different smelling substances on the science table. Blindfold one child and have another hold the jars for the blindfolded child to smell. The blindfolded child tries to guess what he is smelling. Then the two children switch places.

Does It Smell?

Along with a variety of items (lemon, pencil, gum, block, etc.) place two empty boxes on the science table, one labeled "YES" and the other "NO." The children take turns guessing if each item has an odor and placing it in the proper box.

---

v. Taste

Tasting Look Alikes

Ask children to compare the taste of foods that look alike, such as sugar and salt, lemon juice and pineapple juice, water and white vinegar, cola drinks and prune juice, and red pepper and paprika.

Describe the Flavor

Fill four bottles with water. To create the four main taste categories (sweet, sour, salty and bitter) add a little sugar to one bottle, a little lemon juice to the second, a little salt to the third, and a little cough medicine to the fourth. Give each child his or her own cup. One bottle at a time, have the children pour a small amount of the liquid it contains into their cups and taste it. Ask them to describe the taste.

Cooking

Let cooking be optional with the children. Make other activities available for those children who are not interested. For those children who cook, keep the recipes simple. Let everyone eat the finished product.

Surprise Soup

Ask the children to each bring in a vegetable to make "surprise soup." The teacher will probably want to bring a package of dried vegetable soup and seasonings, plus an onion, potato, celery stalks and a can of tomatoes for those children who forget. Each child cleans and, with assistance, cuts up his or her vegetable. Put all the ingredients in a pot. Add water, salt and pepper. Cover the pot and let the soup simmer slowly throughout the school day. Serve it before the children go home at the end of the day.

Comparative Cooking

The teacher selects one food, such as potatoes, peanuts, eggs, carrots, bread or corn, and cooks it in various ways during one week. For example, if the food selected is potatoes, the teacher will boil them one day, bake them the next, then fry them and finally, cut them into thin slices and broil them. Children decide which method of preparation they like best. The teacher should begin to compile a collection of simple recipes to carry out this system.[1]

Cup Cooking

Children prepare a simple recipe using an "assembly line" technique. Break a recipe down into simple steps and draw a large illustration of each step (including measurements) on posterboard. Prop the illustrations up in order on a long table and set up "stations" with all necessary equipment and utensils in front of each drawing for each step in the recipe. Let each child go through the assembly line and follow the recipe.[2]

Many simple recipes may be broken down and illustrated as shown in the figure. Some suggestions are: pancakes, baking powder biscuits, lemonade, stuffed celery, potato salad, fruit salad, baked apples, apple sauce and chocolate milk.

---

[1]Reprinted from INSTRUCTOR, October 1980. Copyright © 1980 by The Instructor Publications, Inc. Used by permission.

[2]*Cup Cooking*. Individualized Child Portion Recipes by Barbara Johnson, illustrated by Betty Plemons, published by Early Educators Press, P.O. Box 1177, 360 Oak Street, Lake Alfred, Florida 33850.

b. Health

Class Discussion

Ask children to give their ideas on how to stay healthy. Explore all aspects of good health, such as proper rest, balanced diet, exercise, good posture, cleanliness, visits to the dentist and doctor, and adequate clothing. Direct the discussion by asking what could happen if any one of these areas is neglected or lacking.

———————————

Good Posture

Have children sit or walk all bent over for five minutes. Then have them walk or sit with straight backs. Ask them, "Which feels better?"

———————————

Bedtime Chart

Make a bedtime chart from posterboard with four or five columns. Label each column with a specific bed time such as 7:30 or 8:00. Post the chart on the bulletin board. Have the children sign their names under the time they go to bed at night.

———————————

Baby Teeth Experiment

If possible, collect baby teeth from the children. Immerse the teeth in various substances for a week. Soda pop turns them brown; grape juice produces sugar crystals; milk keeps them sound. Ask the children, "What can be learned from this experiment?"

———————————

Clean Hands

Have two children demonstrate the importance of clean hands. Have one child wash his hands thoroughly; make sure the other child's hands are dirty. Give each child a cookie to hold and handle. Have each child place his or her cookie in a sterilized Petri dish. (Petri dishes are inexpensive and are available at surgical supply houses.) Seal the dishes and label each dish appropriately "CLEAN HANDS" or "DIRTY HANDS." In three to five days, have the children check the growth of mold on the cookies. The mold on the cookie touched by dirty hands will be more noticeable.

Have You Brushed Your Teeth? Bulletin Board

The teacher draws a large toothless mouth on posterboard and tacks it to the bulletin board. Keep a supply of paper teeth in an envelope labelled "TEETH" tacked to the board. Each day, the children add a tooth to the smile if they brushed their teeth that morning.

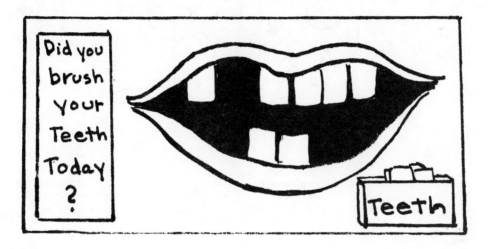

Teeth Charts

Give each child a tooth chart with his or her name on it. (A sample chart is pictured below.) Tape all the charts to the wall or a door. When each child loses a baby tooth, he or she blacks out the corresponding tooth on the chart. The chart is more symbolic than accurate. It is designed to teach concepts rather than facts.

Food Booklets

Discuss the four main classifications of foods: 1) cereals and bread; 2) butter, cheese, and milk; 3) fruit and vegetables; 4) meat, fish and poultry.

Make each child a simple four page booklet out of typing or manila paper. Label each page of each booklet with one of the four food classifications. Have the children draw or cut out of magazines appropriate pictures for each page.

---

2. Animals

There are many ways to categorize animals. They can be divided into the categories of wild animals and domesticated animals. They can also be categorized as animals that fly, walk on land, or live in the water. This book does not attempt scientific classification but presents a variety of activities to supplement any categorization.

Identifying Categories

The teacher holds up a picture of an animal and asks, "What kind of animal is this?" For example, it could be either a mammal, insect, bird, fish, reptile, or amphibian. Children try to guess the category.

---

a. Birds

After a discussion of birds that includes pictures and, if possible, a real nest, have the children dictate a list of bird characteristics which you write on the chalkboard. In addition, you may wish to draw and cut out the outline of a bird and tack it to the bulletin board. Either purchase or have children draw feathers and tack the feathers to the bird outline.

Bird Feeder

Have the children save and decorate empty milk cartons. Cut holes in the cartons for windows. Punch a hole in the "roof" of the feeder and draw a string through it to use to tie the feeder to a tree branch. Put crumbled bread, peanut butter, pumpkin seeds, bird seed, etc., in the feeders and hang them up. If possible, hang the feeders on trees right outside the classroom windows so the children can watch the birds feeding.

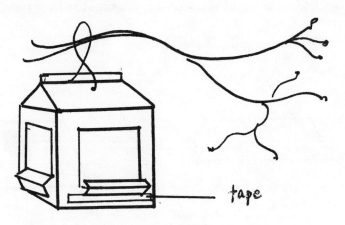

Paper Birds

Give the children bird body patterns to trace and cut out of colored construction paper. Then give them two squares of tissue paper for wings and a tail. Have the children accordian pleat the tissue paper squares and pull them through the slits cut in the bird's body to form side wings and tail feathers.

b. Insects

Discuss harmful and helpful insects. Emphasize body parts and number of legs. Encourage children to bring insects to the classroom to display and discuss.

Spiders

Now that children know that insects have six legs, lead a discussion on spiders. Include illustrations on the chalkboard. Help the children deduce that since spiders have eight legs, they are not true insects.

Make spiders from egg cartons and pipe cleaners.

---

c. Reptiles

Show the children pictures of reptiles such as crocodiles, alligators, snakes, turtles, terrapins, tortoises, lizards, iguanas, and Gila monsters. Ask children to draw their favorite reptile. If they say they can't, demonstrate the following easy snake:

Give each child a large manila paper circle on which you have indicated the beginning of a snake's head, as shown. The children cut the circles into long spirals. Using pictures as models, they decorate their snakes with magic markers.

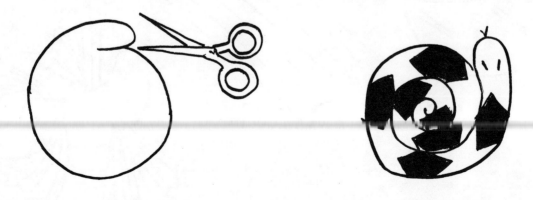

---

d. Fish

Discuss with children which fish may be found in an aquarium and which are in the ocean. If possible, organize a field trip to a pet store to observe the different types of fish.

Give the children basic fish patterns (see pages ___). The children trace, decorate and cut them out. Tack them on the bulletin board and cover the entire board with a large piece of blue cellophane paper.

_____

e. Amphibians

Help the children compare frogs, toads and salamanders. Elicit from the children the one thing these creatures have in common.

Prepare a mimeographed worksheet showing the stages that tadpoles undergo in developing into frogs and toads and give it to the children. Have the children circle the youngest and the oldest figure in the cycle.

_____

A Frog's Life

Lessons on metamorphosis in animals are usually included in the early childhood science program because of the interest they generate. The following exercise may be applied to caterpillars and butterflies as well as frogs.

1. Cut a large circle out of posterboard. Cut out a smaller circle or window near the edge of the large circle.

2. Trace the large circle on mural-sized paper. Inside the edge of the large circle you've drawn, trace the smaller circle you've cut out six times to form six small circles spaced around the edge of the large circle. Draw the six stages of the life cycle of a frog in the six small circles. Tack the mural paper to a bulletin board.

3. Tack the large circle on top of the mural paper, securing it with a single tack in the center which holds the posterboard circle in place but allows it to turn.

First, explain the story and demonstrate the stages of the frog's life by rotating the large circle to expose each of the six pictures in turn. Then allow the children to turn the wheel themselves.

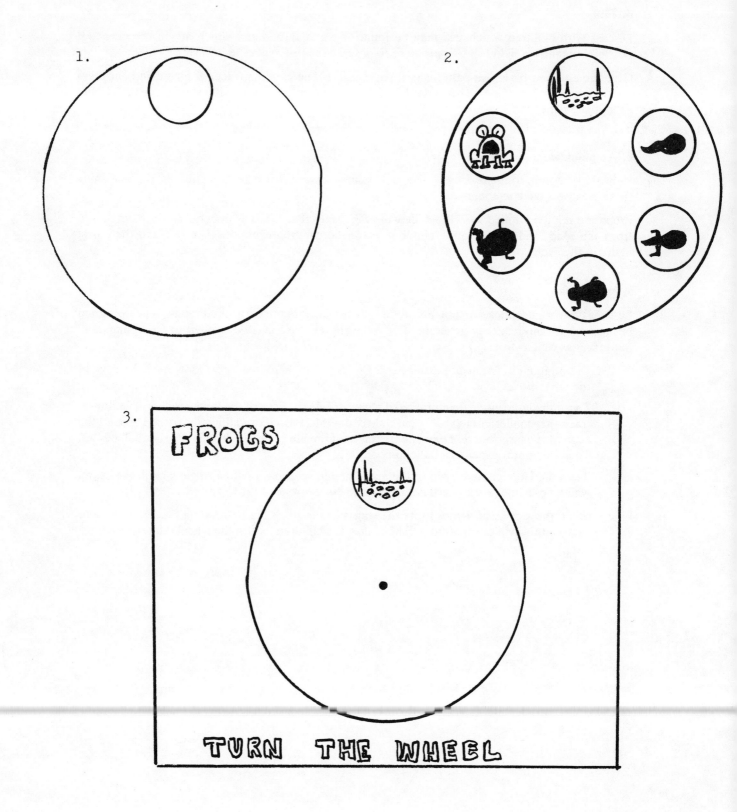

1.

2.

3. FROGS

TURN THE WHEEL

206

f. Mammals

Discuss mammals and their characteristics. If possible, arrange to have a live mammal such as a rabbit or dog at school for the day. Help the children compare mammals with non-mammals such as snakes, turtles, fish and bees.

Animal Chart

Prepare a chart on a large piece of posterboard. Draw in three columns: Pets, Zoo Animals and Farm Animals. Tack the chart on the bulletin board. Give the children stencils of animals to trace and cut out of various colored construction paper. Have the children tape each construction paper animal on the proper column of the chart.

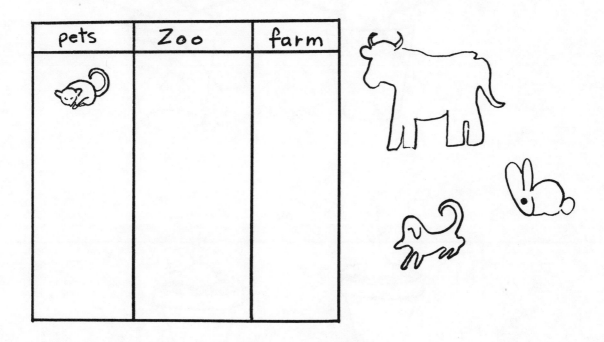

Matching Games With Animals

A variety of picture matching games may easily be constructed and offered in conjunction with study units on animals. Three ideas are:
1. Matching adult animals with baby animals.
2. Matching animals with their footprints (tracks).
3. Matching pictures of animal faces with their ears.

Cut out large pictures of animals. Cut off the animals' ears and glue the ears to posterboard. Cut them out again and back them with Velcro cloth fasteners. Glue the animal faces to large posterboard pieces, leaving enough room to attach the ears.

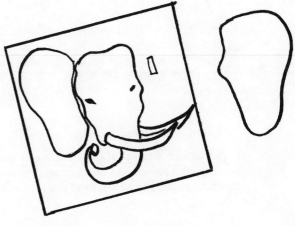

3. Plants

Growing Plants

Plants that are easiest to grow are sweet potatoes, potatoes, onions and avocado seeds. Suspend the potatoes, etc., on toothpicks in a transparent glass, vase or jar filled with water.

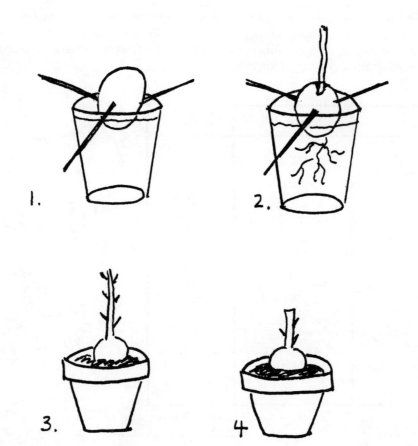

NOTE: Wash the avocado seed first and remove the dry brown covering. Push three toothpicks into the seed. The water in the glass should cover about a half inch of the seed and should not be too cold. When the seed begins to sprout roots it can be potted. Cover most of the seed with dirt. When the plant is about six inches tall, trim approximately four inches off so that the plant will sprout evenly.

Eating Leaves and Flowers

Serve bite sized portions of spinach, cabbage, lettuce, cauliflower and broccoli to the children. If desired, provide the children with mayonnaise or salad dressing to dip the vegetables in. Have the children decide which food is a leaf and which is a flower.

Stems

This activity will demonstrate that stems transport water through the plant. Split a stalk of celery halfway up from the bottom. Put one end in a glass of water to which red food coloring has been added and the other in a glass of water to which blue food coloring has been added. In a few hours the children will be able to observe the movement of the colored water as it travels up into the celery.

Leaves Change Color

All leaves have other colors below the green color. As the days grow shorter in the autumn, children will observe that the green slowly fades away. This experiment illustrates what happens. Use two mason jars. Fill half of one mason jar with bleach. Fill half of the other mason jar with a combination of water and bleach. Put some thick green leaves in each jar, close them tightly, and leave them overnight. The next day, have the children observe what happened.

Seed Bulletin Board

Tack several large drawings of fruits that contain seeds, such as apples, grapes, oranges and grapefruit, on the bulletin board. Have the children bring the appropriate seeds from home and glue them to the drawings.

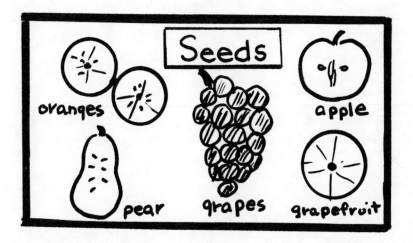

Growing Seeds

Prepare three containers for seeds. Put fertile soil in one container, clay in another and sand in another. Plant the same number and kinds of seeds in each container. Water the seeds and place the containers in a sunny spot. Have the children observe the plants' growth daily.

Musical Play About Plants

One child is the sun and the rest of the class is divided into seeds and raindrops. The teacher accompanies the play with piano or bells.

The seeds are planted. (Children squat on floor.) Softly, drops of rain fall on the seeds. (The raindrops tiptoe through the seeds sprinkling them with their hands.) The sun comes through and shines on the seeds. More rain falls and the seeds grow taller and taller until they turn into beautiful flowers that sway in the breeze. Then everyone dances.

B. THE EARTH

1. Geography

Drawing Maps

Have the children look around the room and see where objects are located. Have the class walk around the room while you call their attention to each area of the room. Give the children manila paper, pencils and crayons and tell them to draw a map of the classroom, placing all furniture in its approximate position.

Placing Objects on a Map

Give children a mimeographed sheet of paper containing an outline of their school. Take them for a walk around the building and ask them to look for trees and to note the trees' placement in relation to the school. Give the children pencils or crayons and have them draw the trees in their proper position on their school maps.

Treasure Maps

Give the children squares of paper cut from brown paper bags. Have the children draw imaginary maps on their pages. Emphasize details with felt marking pens. When the maps are completed, have the children crumple them into a ball, then unfold them and flatten them out again. Give the maps one coat of thin shellac and let them dry. Mount them on colored construction paper. (To make the maps appear older, the teacher can scorch the edges with a lighter or match *before* the maps are shellacked.)

Tracing the Continents

Color maps of the continents with bright marking pens and mount them on oak tag. Give the children tracing paper and crayons to trace as many of the maps as they desire. The children may wish to staple their maps together into booklets.

Continent Puzzle Maps

Montessori schools use large, flat map puzzles with matching outline maps. Each puzzle piece is in the shape of a country and the completed puzzle is in the form of a continent. The outline map also represents the continent but is a simple outline with nothing indicated on the interior. The child first assembles the puzzle in the conventional manner. Then the child fits the countries (the puzzle pieces) into the matching continent outline map and traces the countries in. Labels and small flags often accompany these puzzles. Children can learn to place the proper labels and flags on each country. Older children can place on flags on the location of capitols. Encourage children to trace the countries on blank sheets of paper and label them.

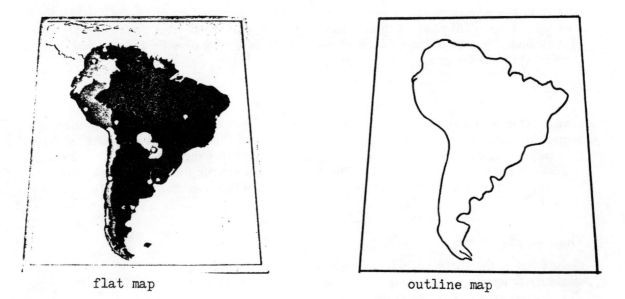

flat map　　　　　　　　　　　　　　outline map

North, South, East and West

The compass points are labelled on the walls of a Montessori classroom. North and south are also indicated on globes and maps. A Montessori teacher often uses a "three point lesson." For example, when demonstrating north and south on a globe, the teacher will say,

    1. "This is the north," pointing to the top of a globe.
    2. (To the child), "Show me the north."
    3. Pointing to the north on the globe, "What is this?"

If possible, provide children with a large simple compass for direction finding outdoors. If a classroom contains a "Playschool Village," the teacher might print in the compass points with a felt marking pen.

Clay Globes

Give each child a pound of clay. Have the children roll the clay into spheres which represent the earth. Have the children flatten the bottom of the globe slightly so it will stand up. Let the clay dry for several days. When it is dry, let each child paint his or her globe blue and tan for water and land. If desired, shellac the globes.

212

Matching Opposites in Nature

Teachers in Montessori schools use contrast cards to teach the natural geographical features of the earth. The teacher prepares the cards in advance. The cards are made on 6" × 8" oak tags and laminated when finished. On each pair of cards, the teacher draws and labels with felt markers pairs of topographical features such as:

> inlet and peninsula
> canyon and mountain
> hills and plains
> lake and island
> cape and bay
> isthmus and strait
> desert and ocean
> forest and prairie
> volcano and crevasse

The child selects one picture card and finds its opposite configuration. The pairs may be numbered for easier matching. Encourage children to identify each picture by name.

Comparing Soil Samples

Give each child one plastic cup. Ask the children to fill their cups with soil found near their homes and bring the cups of soil with them to school the next day. Have the children put the cups of soil on the science table for comparison. These soil samples often reveal a variety of colors and textures.

Finding the Carbonates in Rocks

Fill a glass jar half way with vinegar. Drop rocks, one at a time, into the vinegar. If the rock contains carbonates, it will fizz.

Splitting Rocks

Wrap a rock in a towel and hit it with a hammer. After it is cracked open, let the children examine the rock.

Making a Fossil

Have the children make an imprint in mud with either a leaf or a twig. Let the mud dry and, if possible, bake it. It will get very hard. This activity will illustrate to the children how fossils are formed and why fossilized animal and plant life may be found imbedded in rock.

_____

Classifying Rocks According to Their Hardness

Rocks may be classified according to hardness by simple testing. First the child tests whether a rock can be scratched by a fingernail. If not, the child tests it to see if it can be scratched by a penny. Finally, the child tests it to see if it can be scratched by a file. Have the children separate the rocks into piles by which item scratched it first.

_____

Self-Study

This type of creative self-study is used in the British Infant Schools. Children select their own subject to study and with the teacher's help, prepare a chart suggesting topics to investigate. The following is an example:

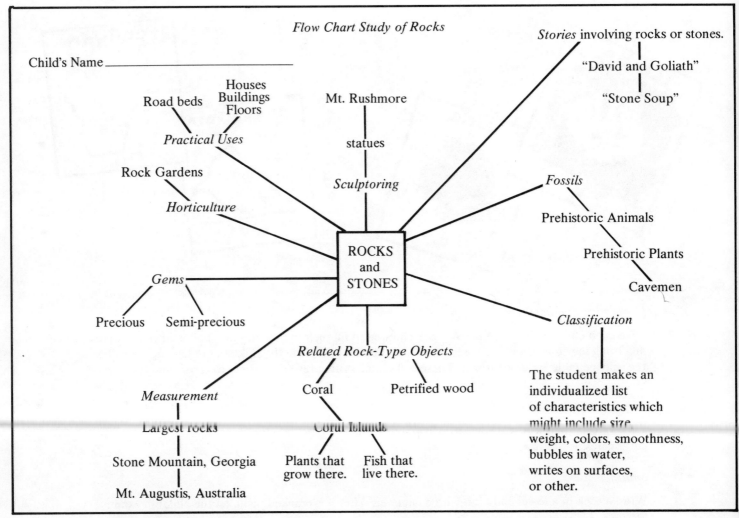

On-going investigations by the student might include written information gathered from research, original poems about rocks, the display of a rock collection, construction of a rock garden, paintings on rocks, etc.

_____

Classifying Shells According to Color

Fill a large box with shells and put it on the science table. At the same time, set up three empty boxes or paper plates, labelled clearly, "WHITE," "BROWN," AND "BLACK." Have the children sort the shells and put them into the proper box or plate.

Making a Volcano

The teacher tapes a 12" × 18" sheet of brown construction paper into the shape of a mountain leaving a hole in the center large enough to accommodate a glass. Fill a glass with vinegar. Put the paper volcano over the glass. Add a little red food coloring. Then add a spoonful of baking soda. The contents of the glass will foam over like a volcano.

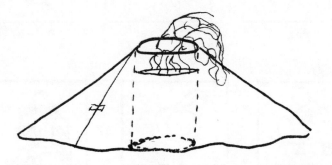

Clean Water

Discuss with the children the importance of clean water. Discuss how water becomes polluted.

Fill several glasses with clean water and place them on the science table, accompanied with small bowls and spoons. Put pollutants such as dirt, soap powder, oil and paint into the bowls. Demonstrate how water becomes polluted when people pour unclean substances into it by putting some of one of the pollutants into one of the glasses of clean water. Let the children experiment by polluting a glass of clean water.

Pollution in the Air

Mount a sheet of white construction paper on a board and cover it with vaseline. Lay the board near a busy street and put a rock in the center. Examine it the next day. The paper will be dirty and the spot where the rock sat will be clean.

Collect Litter

Children make litter bags and then take a walk around the school yard. They collect solid wastes in their bags and when they return to the classroom, they discuss how the litter got on their school yard.

Ecological Chain

The teacher draws on and cuts out from tag board members of a food chain. Back each drawing with felt so that the exercise can be performed on a felt board. Have the children define each picture as you show it to them. Ask them what would happen if one part of the chain were removed.

1 sun

2 rain

3 flower

4 butterfly

5 dragonfly

6 frog

7 snake

8 hawk

2. Weather

Weather Chart

Weather charts may be simple or complicated according to the maturational level of the children who use them. On weather charts illustrate such elements as sun, fog, hail, clouds, rain, frost, lightning, snow, sleet, hurricanes, dust storms and tornadoes. A poster such as the one shown here with an accompanying movable arrow tacked to the center can be adjusted daily by young children to reflect the weather outside.

Windmills

Give children squares of paper, crayons, scissors, a straight pin and a stick or straw. Let them decorate and make their own windmills.

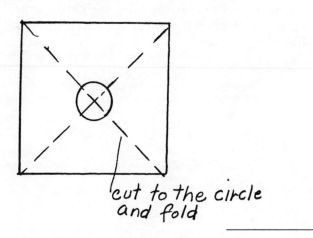

cut to the circle and fold

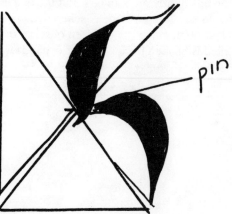

pin

Seasonal Trees

Paint a bare tree on a window or a long piece of butcher paper taped to a wall. During each season have the children decorate it appropriately with leaves, snow, flowers, bird nests, etc.

―――――――――――

Dressing for Weather

Pass around to the children pictures of different articles of clothing. Include snowboots, sweaters, bathing suits, coats, shorts, raincoats, etc. Then, one by one, hold up pictures of different types of weather (sun, snow, rain, etc.) The child holding the picture of clothing fitting the type of weather pictured holds it up.

―――――――――――

Freezing Water

Fill one baby food jar to the top with water. Fill a second baby food jar half way with water. Screw the lids tightly on both jars. Put the jars in an open box outdoors overnight. Be sure that it is a night when the temperature is scheduled to fall below freezing. The next day bring the jars into the classroom. Have the children observe that the water in both jars is frozen but that the jar that was filled is broken because water expands when it freezes.

―――――――――――

Checking the Temperature

Make a thermometer using red and white ribbon and a piece of posterboard as shown in the illustration. Tie an outdoor thermometer outside a school room window. Each day, let a different child read the outdoor thermometer and set the teacher-made thermometer to match the outdoor temperature.

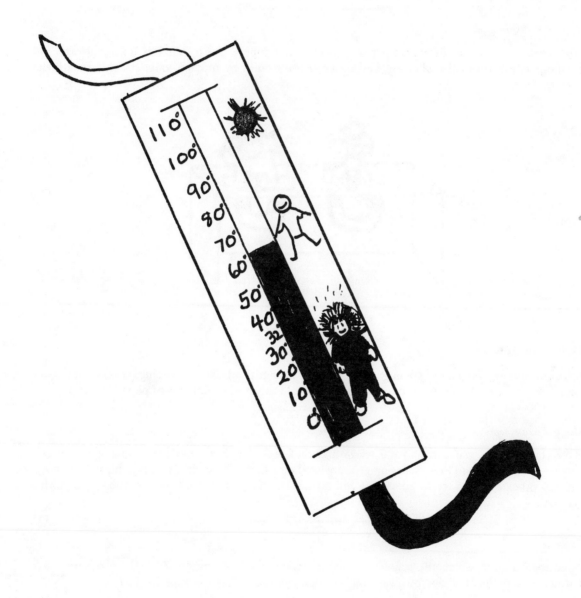

C. FORCES, MATTER AND ENERGY

1. Forces

Magnets

Put a number of steel needles or iron filings on top of a piece of paper. Hold a magnet underneath the paper and move it around. The needles or filings will move as you move the magnet.

Magnetic Puppets

Attach small cardboard cut outs to paper clips to form puppets. Use a shoe box for a platform. Put the puppets on top of the platform and move them around by moving magnets underneath the platform.

Comparing Magnets

Have the children compare two magnets of varying strength and size by hanging paper clips to each one. The one with the stronger magnetic pull will hold the greater number of paper clips.

Magnet Game

Have the children walk around the room and pick up something that they think will attract a magnet. They return to the discussion group with their object. Each child displays his or her object and the other children try to guess if it will attract the magnet. Then they test the object with a magnet.

Pulleys

Have the children watch the school flag being raised in the morning. Have them observe that, because of a pulley, pulling *downward* on the rope causes the flag to move *upward*.

Wagons

Have two or more children move a heavy load of blocks from one corner of the room to another. Then have them move the same load back to its original location using a wagon. Let them decide which task was easier and which took longer.

Levers

Lean a ruler against a small flat object so that at least two inches of one end of the ruler are raised above the table. Put a small light object on the end of the ruler resting on the table. Have the children take turns hitting the raised end of the ruler. They will observe that hitting the raised end of the ruler causes the object to fly through the air.

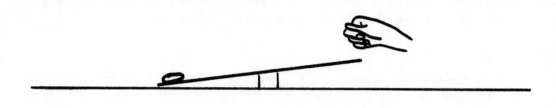

2. Matter

Water Has a Skin I

As the children observe, drop several drops of water onto a piece of waxed paper with an eye dropper. Have the children describe the drops. Have one child touch the drops with a small piece of soap. The children will observe that the skin of the drops breaks and the drops spread out.

Water Has a Skin II

Put water in a dish. Balance a needle on the end of a fork and roll it slowly onto the water. It will float. Have the children observe that if they or the teacher push the needle down, the skin of the water will break and the needle will sink.

Water Is In The Air

Fill a jar with ice and cover it. Have the children observe that soon drops of water form on the outside of the jar.

Cold Water is Heavy

Fill a glass bowl with warm water. Fill a small bottle with cold water. Add a little food coloring to the cold water. Do not cap the bottle. While the children watch, slowly lower the bottle sideways into the warm water. The cold water will sink.

Water and Oil Don't Mix

Pour a little oil into a clear glass. Add water. The children observe that the water will not mix with or dissolve into the oil, even when the liquids are stirred with a spoon.

―――――――

Water Has Weight

Weigh cotton, sponges or other absorbent material before and after immersing the material in water. Discuss with the children the reason for the increase in weight.

―――――――

Salt Water Is Denser Than Fresh

Place an egg in a glass of water. Observe that the egg sinks. Add handfuls of salt to the glass of water until the egg rises to the surface. Have the children discuss why it is easier to float in the ocean than in a swimming pool.

―――――――

Some Things Float; Some Things Don't

Place a large pan of water on the science table. Also put several objects on the table such as a ping pong ball, nails, paper, soap, pencils, cotton, blocks and paper clips. The children take turns experimenting to discover which things float and which sink.

―――――――

Evaporation

Dip two paper towels in water. Put one in the sun and the other in the shade. Examine both of them after an hour. Discuss why one is drier than the other.

―――――――

Air Is A Gas

Show the children an empty plastic squeeze bottle. Ask them if anything is in it. Then squeeze the bottle in the children's faces to prove that there is air in it.

―――――――

Catch the Air

Give each child a small plastic bag. Tell them to run and "catch" the air. As the children run with their bags, the bags will puff up with air.

―――――――

Does Fire Need Air?

Light two candles. Put a glass jar over one of them. What happens to the candle? Will it burn without air? Discuss these questions with the children.

―――――――

Plants Need Air

Coat several leaves of live plants with vaseline. After one week, have the children observe that the coated leaves have died or are dying. Discuss what has happened to the leaves.

―――――――

Air Expands and Contracts

Stretch the mouth of a balloon over an empty test tube. Light a candle and use it to heat the bottom of the test tube. Watch the balloon inflate. Rub the sides of the test tube with an ice cube. Observe that, as the air inside the balloon and the test tube cools, the balloon shrinks.

―――――――

Air Has Weight

Put a deflated balloon on each end of a ruler and balance the ruler on an index finger while resting your hand on a table. The ruler balances. Blow up one balloon and tie or tape it to one end of the ruler. The ruler no longer balances. Have the children decide what was added to the blown up balloon to cause the weight difference.

Air Has Pressure

Put a book on top of a balloon. Blow up the balloon and have the children observe that the book rises because the air in the balloon pushes it up.

Heat Rises in the Air

Under close supervision, have children take turns holding a hand near a lighted candle. Have them observe that their hand is not as warm when they hold it near the sides and bottom of the candle as when they hold it over the top of the candle.

Air Will Lift Water

Tape the ends of three straws together as shown. Have the children observe how high water can be sucked up through the straws.

Air Has Force

Fill a glass bowl with water. Stuff a small water glass with four or five paper napkins. Turn the glass upside down and plunge it into the bowl. Make sure the glass is entirely under water. Lift the glass back out. Have the children observe that the napkins are dry. Explain that the air in the top of the glass kept the water out of the glass and kept the napkins dry.

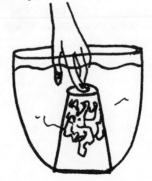

Air Fills Our Lungs

Attach the mouth of a balloon over one end of a long plastic tube. Blow into the tube. The balloon expands. Explain that this is what happens to our lungs when we breathe air.

––––––––––––––––––

3. Energy

Static Electricity

Have the child hold a piece of paper in his or her hands while dragging his or her feet over the rug on a cold day. Have the child press the paper to a wall and see what happens. Due to static electricity, the paper will stick to the wall when placed against it.

––––––––––––––––––

Does Friction Make Heat?

Give each child a 3" square of sandpaper and a small block of wood to rub. Have the children rub the sandpaper on the wood vigorously. Discuss with the children whether or not their fingers feel warm after the period of vigorous rubbing and why.

––––––––––––––––––

A Complete Circuit

Use a 1½ or a 3 volt dry cell battery and uncoated copper wire for the following experiments:

1. Attach a separate wire to each of the terminals on the battery. Wrap the free end of Wire #1 around the bottom of a flashlight bulb. Have the children watch while you touch Wire #2 to base of the bulb and the bulb lights up.
2. Repeat the same experiment with a bell instead of the light. It will ring when the circuit is completed.

If you wish, mount this experiment on a 12" X 12" wooden board and keep it intact for repeated use.

––––––––––––––––––

Combustion

Oxygen combined with certain materials causes combustion, or burning, which is a form of energy. Candles, paper, leaves, wood, straw, etc., will all burn.

A good time to demostrate that fire needs air is at Halloween. After cutting off the top of a pumpkin, scoop out its insides. Before carving out a mouth and eyes, put a candle in the pumpkin and light it. Put the top of the pumpkin back in place Have the children observe that the candle goes out. Now carve out the eyes and mouth and put the candle back in and light it. Put the top of the jack-o-lantern back on. Show the children that the candle now burns. Discuss why.

D. THE UNIVERSE

The Sun Affects Plant Life

Plant and cultivate two similar plants in the classroom. Keep one in the sun and the other in the shade. Children observe the plants' growth each day. If it varies, discuss why.

———————————

The Earth Moves

Outline the shadow of a chair or table in chalk on the floor at the beginning of the school day. Have the children observe the outline and the position of the shadow an hour later. The shadow has moved. Discuss the position of the earth to the sun.

———————————

Measuring Shadows

At the beginning of a sunny day, take the children outdoors. Have the children pair up and measure their partner's shadow. Later on in the day, have the partners measure each other's shadow again. Note how the shadows have changed.

———————————

Experimenting With a Doll's Shadow

With the classroom lights turned off, children experiment with a flashlight and a doll to produce the doll's shadow. Have the children hold the flashlight in various positions relative to the doll (in front of the doll, directly over its head, etc.), and measure the shadows created. Compare the flashlight to the sun.

———————————

Blast Off

The teacher blows up a balloon very taut and then releases it while the children observe. Discuss the concept that rockets push through space in much the same manner although their direction is controlled.

———————————

226

Moon Men or Astronauts

Discuss with the children why men could walk on the moon and not on the sun. Have children make astronaut helmets with round half gallon ice cream containers, cellophane and pipe cleaners. Turn the containers upside down. Attach two pipe cleaners to the bottom (now the top) of each ice cream container. Cut a window out of the container and staple colored cellophane inside.

Remembering the Planets

At the Fernbank Science Center in Atlanta, Georgia, children are given the following sentence to help them remember the names of the planets in order of their proximity to the sun:

<u>M</u>y <u>V</u>ery <u>E</u>ducated <u>M</u>other <u>J</u>ust <u>S</u>erved <u>U</u>s <u>N</u>ine <u>P</u>izzas

The first letter of each word is the same as the first letter in each of the planets:

<u>M</u>ercury
<u>V</u>enus
<u>E</u>arth
<u>M</u>ars
<u>J</u>upiter
<u>S</u>aturn
<u>U</u>ranus
<u>N</u>eptune
<u>P</u>luto

Clay Moons

Give each child a half pound of clay. Have the children roll their clay into a sphere. Have the children stamp craters into the surface of the sphere with the blunt end of a pencil. Attach a small American flag to a toothpick and stick the toothpick into the moon to signify a moon landing.

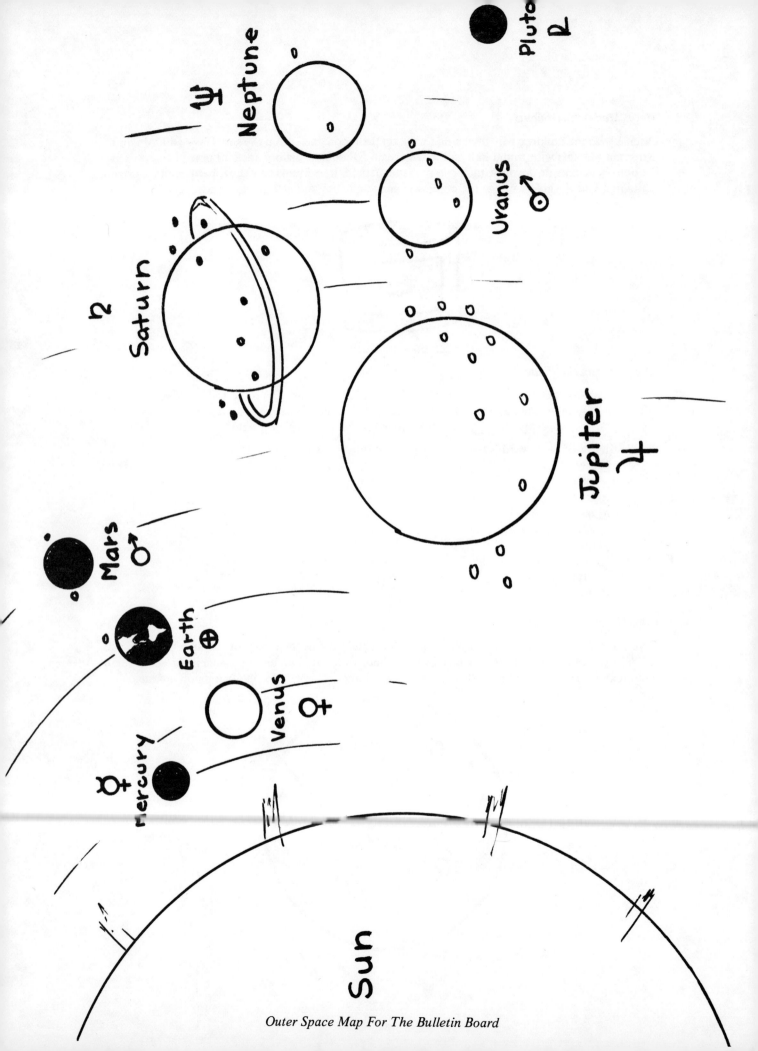

Outer Space Map For The Bulletin Board

Plotting the Constellations

Display several constellation charts on the bulletin board. Put a supply of dark construction paper, chalk, glue, string and gummed silver stars on a nearby table. Have the children create constellations with the materials supplied, copying those displayed. Let the children make as many as they want. If desired, staple each child's constellations together to form a booklet.

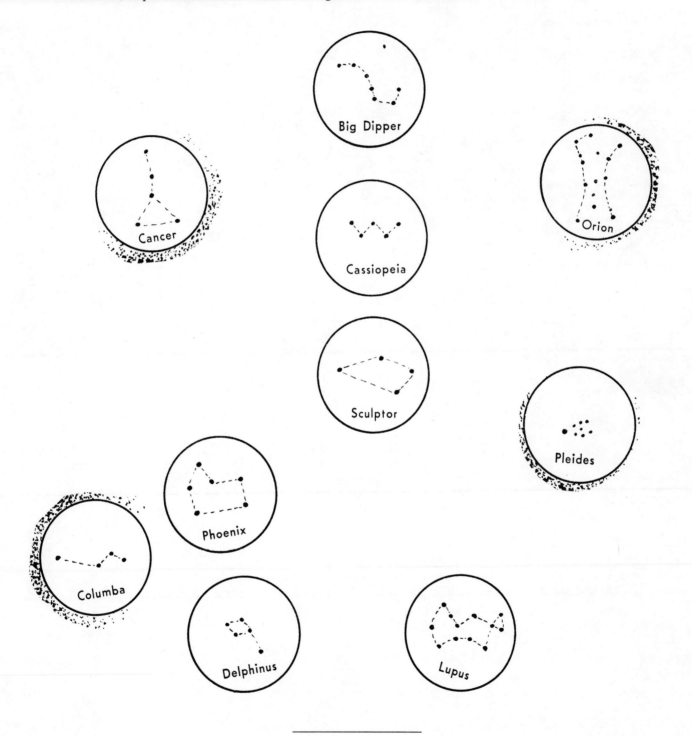

The Solar System

Montessori schools have an ellipse taped to the floor which is called their walking line. The children use the walking line to demonstrate the planets rotating around the sun. A lighted candle placed in the center of the ellipse represents the sun and nine children, each carrying a picture of one of the nine planets, walk the line.

Social studies is concerned with the relationship between people and their social and physical environment. Since the environment is constantly changing, the social studies curriculum varies from year to year and from text to text. This reference book attempts to include those areas which are particularly pertinent to young children.

A. SELF-CONCEPTS

If children learn positive feelings about themselves when they are young, they have a better chance of succeeding in future learning situations. The activities described here were selected because they are directed toward fostering healthy self-images.

Sociograms

Often teachers would like to know how each child fits into the social patterns within the classroom. Sociometric data are direct reflections of interpersonal relationships and sociograms are the most frequently used method to obtain this information. The teacher asks each child (privately) a question related to choosing a friend in the room such as: "Who would you like to invite home with you?" or "Who would you like to sit near during snacktime?" The teachers chart the children's answers (see illustration below) which reveal who the leaders are, who belongs to social groups, and who is omitted. In this way, a teacher can subtly choose activities which promote interaction among all the children and involvement of the child who tends to be excluded or left out.

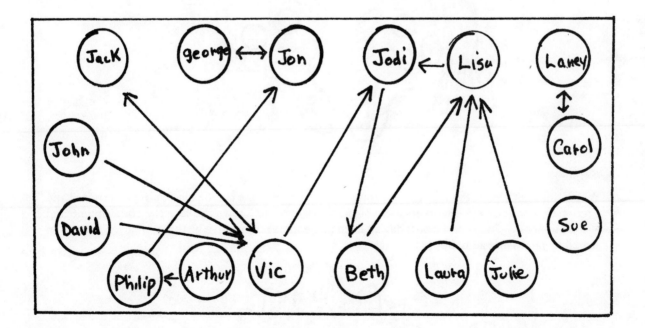

"The Wendy House"

British Infant Schools have a playhouse set up in an area of one room called "The Wendy House" in which children are free to make believe. Costumes, blocks, small pieces of furniture, and other accessories are added at different times for variety. Often a shy child will assume a fictitious role in "The Wendy House," overcoming self-conscious feelings.

Self-portraits

Self-portraits are often revealing, especially when the child is given instructions to draw an action picture such as, "Draw yourself playing with your best friend," or "helping your mother with the baby," or "feeding your pet," etc.

ME Booklets

In the course of a week, give children a variety of subjects to draw. The subjects might include self-portraits, family portraits, pets, the child's home, handprints, footprints, addresses, telephone numbers, favorite toys, etc. The teacher keeps the children's drawings and staples them together at the end of the week. Colored constuction paper may be decorated and used as a cover to make the booklet appear more important. Send the booklets home with the children.

Family Face Puppets

The teacher makes life-sized faces from posterboard backed with cardboard to keep them sturdy. Make faces of family members such as mother, father, grandparents, sister, brother, and baby. Cut out the eyes in each face to allow visual contact with others when the children use the faces as masks.

Birthdays

When children have birthdays, they enjoy wearing crowns. These can be cut out of posterboard and decorated with felt tipped markers and glitter. Make sure the crown displays the child's name and age prominently. To make the birthday an even more special time, give birthday children priority in selecting games and activities for the day.

Pretend Birthday Cakes

Use a round ice cream carton for a pretend cake. Have the children whip up some fluffy soapsuds and frost it. Tinted macaroni, plastic leaves, etc., may be used to trim the cake. Top the cake off with candles.

Birthday Bulletin Boards

Ideas for making birthday charts and birthday bulletin boards are endless. Trees, balloons, lollipops, flowers, ships, flags, birds, butterflies, etc., each can be labelled with the name of a month and children's birthdays printed on them. The following cake may be tacked on a wall.

Birthday Trains

The birthday train may be tacked on or above a bulletin board and kept all year. Children also enjoy tracing an engine and cars which they decorate and take home.

Montessori Birthday Histories

Before a child's birthday, the teacher contacts his/her parents and obtains pertinent information about the child's background, such as birthplace, brothers and sisters, trips taken, favorite toys, special relatives, pets, and preferred activities. If possible, parents contribute photographs for the occasion. The teacher fashions the information and photographs into a booklet about the birthday child. After reading the booklet to the group, the teacher gives it to the child as a memento.

In the event a booklet is not possible, tell the child's story to the group and pass the photographs around. You may wish to supplement the story with simple chalkboard drawings (see the illustration below).

Happy Birthday, Merle

mommy and daddy   my dog   my best toy   I like the circus

_____

Child's History as Depicted in a Montessori Time Line

Record the important events of a child's life (such as birth, first house or apartment in which he/she lived, family automobile, etc.) on a long, narrow piece of sturdy paper or canvas-type material. List all facts in chronological order, illustrated with photographs or simple drawings. Encourage the child to follow the story with you in sequence, which will promote a sense of personal history.

_____

Sign Up Bulletin Boards

Prepare sign up bulletin boards which require children to think and make selections. For example, prepare a board which asks children to select a favorite item from among many items pictured, or a favorite color from among many colors. Keep pencils handy for use at the sign up board.

Helping Hands Chart

Make a Helping Hands chart with columns or boxes labelled with the various classroom tasks to be done. Prepare construction paper hands. Label each one with the name of a child in the class. As the teacher assigns a daily or weekly job to a child, he/she tacks or tapes the hand labelled with that child's name in position on the chart.

Wish Booklets

Have children draw pictures or write what they would like to have or do, where they would like to go, etc. Staple each child's papers together to form a booklet. Let the child prepare a construction paper cover labelled "My Wish Book."

Our Bunch

Draw a large bunch of grapes on posterboard. Paste a picture of each chilid in the center of each grape.

The Whole Blooming First Grade (or Kindergarten, etc.)

Draw a large bouquet of daisies. Paste a picture of each child in the center of each daisy.

News Bulletin

Children dictate their news to the teacher and he/she transcribes it on a chart tablet. Either keep the news bulletin on the chart tablet or tack it to the bulletin board.

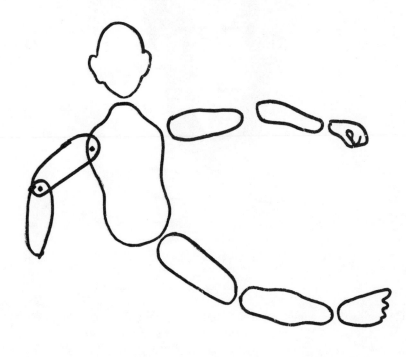

Parts of the Body

The teacher cuts out body parts from pieces of different colored felt for children to assemble on a felt board. An alternative activity is to provide children with cardboard patterns of these same body parts. The children trace the parts, cut them out and put them together with brads to make a puppet. Help the children learn to identify each body part.

Left Hand, Right Hand Identification

Each child traces and cuts out his/her right hand and left hand. Use one color of construction paper for the right hand and a different color for the left hand.

Measuring Height

Taping a measurement chart to a wall or door in September and measuring children at their request during the year can give them an indication of growth patterns. Make a posterboard figure and make a felt measuring strip to attach to the posterboard figure. Make sure the 3' mark on the measuring strip is accurately measured from the floor. In September, give each child a clothespin labelled with his or her name. Use it to indicate each child's height by attaching it to the appropriate point on the measuring strip. The pins can be moved easily as the children grow.[1]

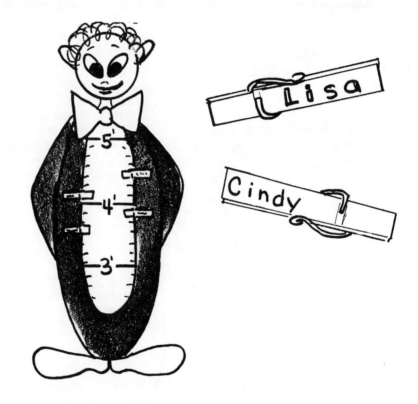

---

1. Elaine Commins, "Growing Up." Reprinted with permission from the publisher, Allen Raymond, Inc., Darien, CT. 06820. From the April 1981 issue of *Early Years*.

Personal Charts

Charts such as the one pictured below call for information about the child and require the child to decide what response is appropriate, and to indicate his or her decision by writing his or her name in the proper column. As an alternative, the teacher can provide construction paper figures to accompany the chart, which the child will sign and tape or tack in the appropriate column instead of simply signing the chart. Topics for charts might include types of dwelling (houses or apartments), how many brothers and sisters in a family, whether the child can swim or skip or hop, etc. At times it may be appropriate for a child to sign more than one column.

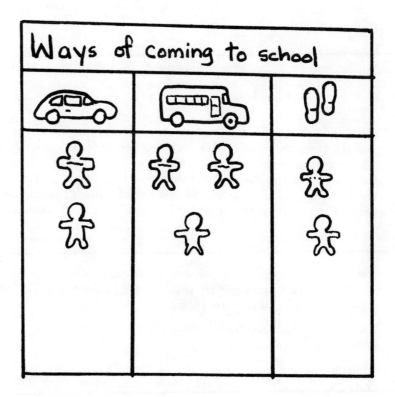

Family Structure

The teacher arranges various family groupings with felt board characters, each one different. For instance, some groupings will include a father and some not; some a mother and some not, etc. Have the children verbally identify a particular group as representative of their family. After a class discussion, let each child manipulate the characters in turn. This activity presents an opportune time for the teacher to explain that many mothers and fathers don't live in the same house or apartment. Often a child caught up in a divorce situation finds comfort in knowing that other children are faced with the same problem. As a further activity, children enjoy drawing their family, including pets, for a bulletin board display. If a child includes imaginary relatives in his or her picture, accept them without question.

Role Playing I

The teacher suggests problems and each child is given a turn to act them out. Some ideas of problems for role playing are

"How would you act if you were the only child in the class who didn't get a Valentine?"

". . . if you were afraid to go to bed at night because you didn't like the dark?"

". . . if you didn't want to paint a picture because you were afraid that the other children might laugh at you?"

". . . if you were trying to do homework and your sister or brother keeps bothering you?"

". . . if you were buying some candy and you forgot your money?"

Role Playing II

Give children puppets to use for dramatization. Each puppet has a characteristic name such as "hitter," "pusher," "cry-baby," "loudmouth," "giggles," or "runny-nose."

Emotions

Have children stand in two lines, about five feet apart facing each other so that each child faces a partner. Have each pair of children symbolize opposite emotions. For instance, one is happy, and his/her partner is sad. The teacher calls on one couple at a time to act out their emotions as they walk toward each other. As they pass each other, the partners exchange emotions. For instance, the happy child becomes sad and the sad child becomes happy. Other opposites are confident/shy, peppy/sluggish, friendly/unfriendly, mean/sweet, careful/careless, hungry/full, and nervous/calm.

Mirrors

Two children face each other. One makes movements with his/her face, arms, legs, or body and the second child copies or "mirrors" the movements. After a few minutes, they exchange roles and the second child initiates the movements.

Friendly Walk-Around

Sometime during the day, the teacher calls for a break in the activities. He or she beats a tom-tom or claps, 1-2-3. The children take three steps and after the third beat, they stop, smile, and pose while saying "hello" to a neighbor. They then change directions, take three more steps to the teacher's beat and say "hello" to a new neighbor.

Descriptions

Children and teacher sit in a circle. One child at a time describes another child without mentioning clothing. This activity encourages children to delve into the personalities, such as likes and dislikes, and the physical attributes of their classmates.

Acting Out Social Courtesies

Using equipment in the room, children take turns answering the telephone, introducing people, answering the door, thanking someone for passing out cookies, etc.

Letter Writing (Grades 1 through 3)

Have children exchange names and write letters to each other.

Tape Recorder Interview (Grades 1 through 3)

Have one child pretend to be a reporter and interview another child, asking the "interviewee" questions about pets, birthdays, number of brothers and sisters, where the child has lived, etc.

Class Movies

Movies taken of a class are an excellent means of social reinforcement. Give each child an equal role in the film. Run the film forward and backward for the children's amusement.

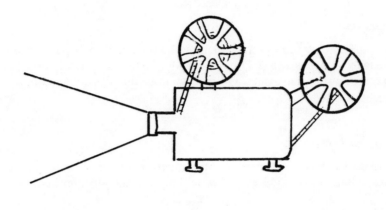

Practical Tasks

Montessori philosophy believes that very young children should be grounded securely in reality before they venture into make-believe and fantasy. Provide children exercises in "practical life" such as polishing, pouring, washing, folding, zipping, buckling, buttoning, sweeping, and brushing. Be developing competence in performing useful tasks, children improve muscular coordination as well as gaining positive feelings of accomplishment.

B. THE COMMUNITY

Neighbors, community workers, religious institutions and various ethnic groups make up the community.

What Do They Do?

Give children paper, pencils, and crayons and tell them to draw a picture of what daddy does all day and a picture of what mother does all day. Parents usually appreciate these pictures when they come visit for PTA meetings.

_____

Charting Various Occupations

Using a chart tablet, the teacher records a list dictated by the children of persons who work in the community. The teacher either draws simple figures which illustrate the children's suggestions or the children cut pictures out of magazines and tape them to the chart. The children's list may be longer than you might expect.

_____

Visiting Community Workers

If possible, ask workers such as a mailman, a policeman, a plumber, or a construction worker to spend a few minutes talking to the children and describing specific jobs that they do.

_____

Matching the Person with the Profession

The teacher pastes or draws pictures of workers such as doctor, dentist, nurse, beautician, butcher, baker, sheriff, cowboy, policeman, pilot, or TV cameraman on 4" × 6" oak tags. The teacher also prepares accompanying cards containing pictures of tools used in each profession pictured on the oak tags. Have the children match the pairs.

_____

Guess My Profession

Children take turns acting out specific occupations while the rest of the class guesses what they are.

Riddles

The teacher makes up riddles describing an occupation and the children try to guess what it is. For example:

> He wears a blue uniform.
> He drives a car with the steering wheel on the wrong side.
> He brings letters to your house.
> Who is he?

Make the clues successively easier.

Build a Skyscraper

Have each child bring a cardboard box from home. The teacher furnishes large boxes. The children paint the boxes and stack them on top of each other to make a large building. If desired, tape them together so that they hold more permanently.

Trip to the Post Office

Use a trip to the post office to enhance other learning experiences such as writing to a sick child, inviting parents to the school, thanking someone for being nice to the children, etc.

Acting Out Occupations

Through dramatic play the young child integrates experiences. To stimulate interest, make an area of the room accessible for play acting and furnish it with accessories. The following job suggestions are sure to open up new opportunities for creative drama:

> bus driver, shoemaker, painter, farmer, mailman, clerk, doctor, nurse, plumber, telephone repairman, gardener, waitress, gas station attendant, pilot, stewardess, singer, dancer, musician

---

Beauty Parlor and Barber Shop

Give each child a 12" × 18" piece of construction paper to decorate. The teacher then staples the ends together to form a head covering. Use some as bonnets and tape a few to the wall to serve as hair dryers. Put chairs below each "dryer" for customers to sit in.

Provide accessories such as combs, a hand mirror, hair curlers, a cordless curling iron, striped barber aprons, and tongue depressors for shaving the boys. Given a free rein, children will play-act their roles eagerly.

Comparing Religions

Religion is a controversial subject only to adults. By treating all religions with interest and respect, the teacher will insure that children will enjoy the subject and that no one will feel uncomfortable. The most practical method of introducing various religions to young people is to celebrate a variety of religious holidays. Another method is to visit a church, a cathedral, a synagogue, or a mosque. Try to arrange to have a guide from each house of worship give the class a tour and answer questions and explain in simple terms a little of the philosophy of that religion.

Differing Ethnic Groups

America's original inhabitants, as well as the oldest and the newest immigrants, are of great interest to all children. If the class has children whose parents or grandparents came from other lands, try to persuade them to visit the school and display native costumes, foods, music, etc. In one experimental school, children were asked to select one culture and pretend they were part of it for the entire quarter's work. The children selected American Indians and they studied Indian music, dancing, art, crafts, science, nature study, literature, dress, food, construction skills, physical education, etc. This activity was based on the belief that children can understand a different culture best by making it their own.

All American Bulletin Board

When engaged in a study unit devoted to the various cultures which make up America, prepare a multi-cultural bulletin board as shown here:

Cut the parts from large pieces of colored construction paper and tack them to the bulletin board. You can also make small cardboard figures of the "all Americans" pictured on the bulletin board display. Prepare environment cards which picture various natural settings found in America, such as a big city, farm, desert, village, mountains, or sea shore. Have the children take turns placing the cardboard figures in the appropriate environmental setting.

Festivals or Celebrations

Montessori schools incorporate days of celebration in their cultural geography program. The class finishes a unit of study of the people in a foreign country with a festival. Participation by parents as well as outside interested parties is encouraged. The following are examples:

Christian: Christmas, Easter

Jewish: Passover, Hanukkah, Purim, Succos

Moslem: Ramadan

Hindi: The Winter Festival of Lights

Druids: Winter Solstice

Halloween: International Childrens Day (everyone dresses in a traditional costume from another country)

International Dinner: an international potluck dinner

Africa Festival: folk dances, preparing a typical meal, making model houses, etc.

———————————

Collections

Have the class start a scrapbook of postcards, stamps, money, etc., from other lands. When each child brings an item for the scrapbook to school, he/she shows it to the others and describes it. Then he/she pastes it into the scrapbook in the proper place. (If the children wish to take their possession home, they can "lend" it to the scrapbook, a book with cellophane pages which stick to the backing, for a few weeks and then take it home.)

———————————

C. TRANSPORTATION AND COMMUNICATION

Transportation and communication involve moving ideas, things, and people from one location to another.

Walk On Maps

Tape pathways on the floor with masking tape. Use blocks and safety signs to indicate signals and buildings. In addition, tape drawings by children of houses, trees, cars, etc., on the floor. Encourage children to engage in free exploration of the area.

Vacation Map

Ask children to tell the class where they are going or where they would like to go on a vacation. Tack a large map, surrounded by cards bearing the children's names, to the bulletin board. Use pieces of string to connect the child with the selected vacation spot.

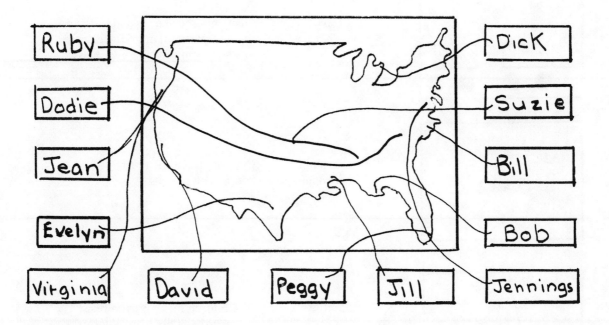

Worksheets on Measuring Distances (Grades 2 and 3)

Give children worksheets in which they fill in the number of inches or centimeters on a map between cities, rivers, continents, etc.

Transportation Booklets

Give the children a different written exercise to complete each day. Keep the children's pages until the end of the week and then staple each child's papers together to form a booklet. The exercises may include painting, pasting, coloring, and, for the older child, written answers. The following are ideas for the transportation booklet:

Transportation Booklet

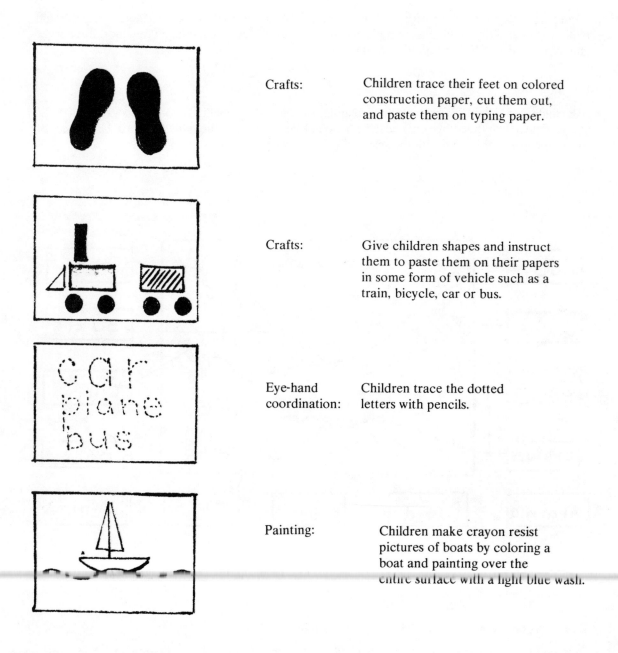

Crafts: Children trace their feet on colored construction paper, cut them out, and paste them on typing paper.

Crafts: Give children shapes and instruct them to paste them on their papers in some form of vehicle such as a train, bicycle, car or bus.

Eye-hand coordination: Children trace the dotted letters with pencils.

Painting: Children make crayon resist pictures of boats by coloring a boat and painting over the entire surface with a light blue wash.

Visual-discrimination exercise:

Ask children to circle all the objects that are some means of transportation.

You can go far in a _____.
You can float in a _____.
You can ride in the rain in a _____.

Auditory Discrimination Exercise:

Children finish the rhymes by printing or drawing their answers.

Safety Signs

Teach children the meaning of a selected number of safety signs. Emphasize the signs' configurations. Have the children trace, color and cut out safety signs on oak tag. Then have the children glue finished signs to tongue depressors and mount them in clay stands.

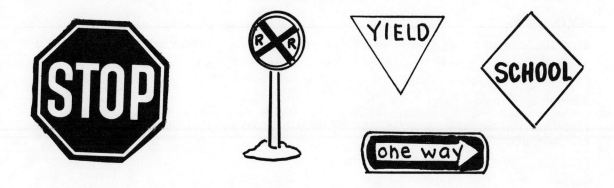

251

Bus Ride Around the City

Children have a cupcake or candy sale and the money earned is spent on taking the entire class on a bus ride around the city.

Communication

Hold a class discussion on how to get a message to someone who is far away.

Mail Box

Children paint a large cardboard carton to resemble a mailbox. They write or type letters to friends in the room. Post a list of the children's names near the mailbox. The children put their letters in envelopes, address the envelopes, and "mail" the letters by putting them in the box. The mail is "delivered" once a week by the teacher or a child.

Stamp Collage

Make a large drawing of a mail box and tack it to a bulletin board. Ask children to bring in cancelled stamps and glue them on a clearly defined area of the box to form a stamp collage. Discuss the differences in the stamps' design and cost.

Class Newspaper

Have the children vote on a title for a class newspaper. Each child contributes at least one sentence to the newspaper which is typed on mimeograph paper by the teacher. After running it off on the mimeograph machine, give each child a copy of the newspaper to take home to give to parents.

Telephone Books

Prepare and give to the children blank books in the shape of a telephone. List all the children's telephone numbers on a chart tablet. Have the children copy the names and phone numbers of the other students off the chart tablet into their telephone books.

TV Programs

Have the children dictate a list of favorite TV programs and/or commercials and record it on a chart tablet. Have the children count the number of programs listed.

Charting TV Program Times

Prepare a chart on which children can record the time of day and stations on which their favorite programs appear.

D. ECONOMICS

The buying, selling, producing, and consuming of goods and services are all intrinsic parts of our culture. Very young children can be introduced to elementary economic concepts.

Money

Have children make their own money. "Price" certain toys and put them on a special table or tables. Provide a money box for each table. The children use their play money to pay for playing with the toys contained on the special table(s). At the end of the day, collect the money boxes and count the money.

Inflation

Explain to children that during inflation, people must spend a greater number of dollars to buy the things that they need. Blow up a balloon and paste play dollars all over it. Have the children decide if it takes a greater number of dollars to cover the balloon when it is inflated or when it is not.

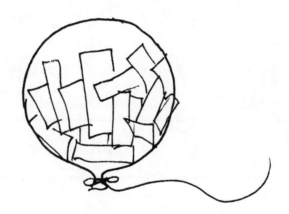

Coin Rubbings

Give children coins to observe. Call their attention to the engravings on the coins. Have the children cover the coins with typing paper and make rubbings with colored crayons.

Savings

Have the children decide on a money raising project such as a paper sale or collecting bottles and taking them to the grocery store for deposit money. Take the children to the bank. Open a savings account with all the money earned. The class will receive a bank book. Keep it available for children's examination at any time.

Game of "Where Do We Buy?"

Ask the children where we buy various items such as bread, candy, gasoline, medicine, apples, coats, dolls, toothpaste, records, or bicycles. Children try to answer each question.

A Mountain of Wants

People have desires or needs for goods and services. Give children magazines and have them cut out pictures of articles or services that they would like to have. Draw an outline of a mountain on the bulletin board. Have the children fill in the mountain with their pictures.

Creating a Store

Create a store with large building blocks. Have the children bring empty food cartons to school, such as milk cartons, gelatin boxes, cereal boxes, empty tin cans, egg cartons, spaghetti boxes and cake mix boxes. Provide a cash register, play money, and shopping bags. Let the children play store. Introduce them to the terms "producers" and "consumers."

Blueprints

Have children pretend that they are workers in a car factory. Give them blue paper and white chalk to design new cars. The teacher makes play money in $1.00 and $10.00 denominations. Pay children $1.00 for every design and $2.00 for an especially good one. At the end of the school day, the children add up their income and take home their earnings.

E. HISTORY

Introduce young children to historical concepts by means of discussions of holidays and comparisons of the old with the new. Chronological events are beyond the intellectual grasp of most children at this age so dates should be avoided.

Columbus Day

Tell the story of Columbus' discovery of America, using pictures to illustrate important segments. Then give children boat patterns to trace on manila paper, and let them paint or color them.

Sea Monster Pictures

Remembering the fears of Columbus' sailors, the children color sea monster pictures with crayons, then wash over them with pale blue paint.

Indian Teepees

Each child traces a teepee pattern on 12" × 18" manila paper. After the teepee is decorated and cut out, staple three or four straws to the straight edge as shown, and fold the teepee around them. Staple the edges together.

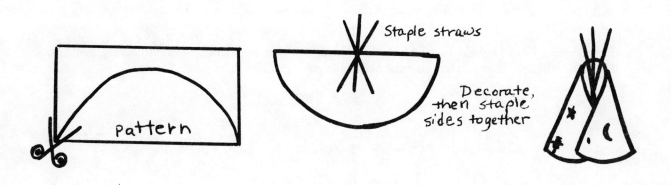

Indian Papoose

Children cut out a frame from cardboard (for instance, shirt stuffers from laundries) and decorate it. They also draw and cut out a baby's head which they staple to the frame. Punch holes near the top and bottom of both sides of the frame and tie yarn to the holes forming "straps" through which the mother puts her arms to carry the papoose on her back.

Indian Canoes

Have the children fold a piece of paper in half. Give the children a canoe pattern and have them place the bottom edge of the pattern on the fold, trace the canoe, decorate it, and cut it out. Staple or lace at the ends of the canoe.

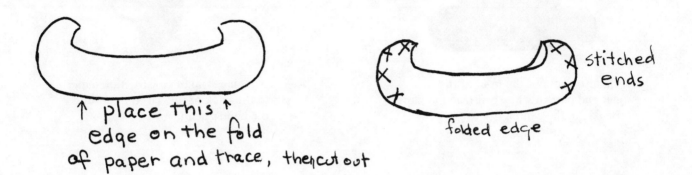

↑ place this ↑
edge on the fold
of paper and trace, then cut out

stitched ends

folded edge

Thanksgiving Food

During the Thanksgiving season, have the children prepare food that might have been cooked by the pilgrims, such as cranberry sauce, squash, sweet potatoes, pumpkin pie, and corn.

Pilgrim Hats

Use white and black or gray construction paper to make pilgrim hats:

Pilgrim Hat Number 1

Paste a strip of white paper to one side of a 12" × 18" piece of black construction paper. Fold on the dotted line.

Fold the two black corners over each other and staple them together.

A white construction paper buckle may be pasted on the front.

257

Pilgrim Hat Number 2

Children cut out the front of the hat and paste a white construction paper buckle in the center.

Attach a strip of construction paper to the back of the hat to fit around the child's head.

Discuss how Pilgrim hats are different from hats people wear today.

_____

Comparing United States Flags

Display several drawings or pictures of different United States flags. The first, adapted in 1777, contained 13 stars. As states were added to the Union, stars were added to the flag. Have the children arrange the flags in chronological order by counting the number of stars on each. The older the children, the more flags to be arranged. Students in second or third grade might also be asked to list the names of states as they were added.

_____

Patriotic Bulletin Board

Cover the bulletin board with a red, white and blue background. Have children draw pictures of George Washington and Abraham Lincoln and tack them up. Change the pictures often. Encourage the children to draw scenes such as Washington chopping down the cherry tree and Lincoln splitting rails.

_____

Comparing the Old with the New

The teacher holds up pictures of old and new things such as old and new cars, boats, telephones, radios, clothing, bicycles, furniture, houses, and schools. Children guess which is old and which is new.

_____

Time Lines

Montessori schools make excellent use of time lines. They usually consist of long strips of durable material on which sequential dates are indicated. The time lines are sturdy enough to be walked on by the children. Some time lines have accompanying material such as model dinosaurs which can be placed in the Mesozoic era and model people which are to be placed in the Cenozoic era. A more modern time line to which American children can relate would indicate Indians, then Columbus, the Pilgrims, Yankee soldiers and Confederate soldiers, then people in clothing of the early 20th century, then soldiers from World War I, etc.

_____

Other Ideas for Montessori Time Lines

1. A time line of the events of a normal school day
2. A time line of a week in school
3. A time line of the year including the seasons, holidays and birthdays

———————————————

F. GOVERNMENT

By treating the classroom as a microcosm of the outside world, the teacher can plan activities to initiate learning which, in time, children can apply to forms in the government.

Class Elections

Teach children to vote with a show of hands on various issues such as field trips, classroom activities, songs to sing, stories to hear, and foods to cook. In addition, have the class elect students to perform monitorial functions.

Government Elections

When an important election is held, hold the same election in the classroom. Tape photographs of the candidates to the chalkboard, and have the children take turns selecting the candidate of their choice by making a mark on the board under the appropriate picture. In the primary grades, have the children use the secret ballot. Construct a voting booth out of cardboard or building blocks and prepare paper ballots. Put a picture of each candidate, labelled with his or her name, on each voting booth.

Class Discussions

Discuss the nation's highest elected positions. Ask the children to define terms such as "President," "Vice-President," "Senator," and "Governor." Often their definitions are curiously accurate.

Class Constitution

Have the children make up their own rules for the classroom. Let each child suggest a rule, no matter how trivial. The teacher writes down the children's rules under the heading "Class Constitution." Tape the Class Constitution to the wall.

Field Trip

Following preliminary discussions and activities, take the children to visit city hall.

Listing Federal and Local Government Jobs and Agencies

Help the children make a list which names the jobs and agencies connected with the government. Write the list on the chalkboard or a chart tablet.

President	Army	Health dept.
Vice-president	Navy	Welfare dept.
Governor	Marines	City parks
Lt. Governor	Air Corps	Schools
Senator	Coast Guard	Library
Congressman	Post Office	Highways
Mayor	Space Program	Hospitals
Sheriff		Police dept.
Teacher		Fire dept.
		Water works
		Street lights
		Traffic lights
		Sanitation dept.

Who Pays?

Discuss with the children who pays the President's salary, the soldier's salary, the policeman's salary, etc. Discuss what would happen if no one paid taxes.

Other Kinds of Government

Discuss with the children what would happen if people were not allowed to vote for a president. What kind of government would they have then?

Recognizing Government Buildings and Monuments

Show children a collection of photographs of important government buildings and monuments, such as the Capitol, White House, Pentagon, U.S. Treasury, Washington Monument, Lincoln Memorial, Jefferson Memorial, and Arlington National Cemetery. Use state as well as federal buildings. As you hold up each picture, have the children try to guess the identity of the building or monument it represents.

Have children trace patterns of well known monuments and paste them on a mural. They may paint in foliage to add to the mural's effectiveness.

WE'LL HELP YOU TO HELP THEM.

EDUCATION

108-80 LOOKING AT CHILDREN. Richard Goldman, Ph.D.; Johanne Peck, Ph.D.; Stephen Lehane, Ed.D. Combines theory and practice, exploring such issues as language development, classification, play and moral development in children. Also includes a look at sex typing, television, single-parent families, and the fathers role in parenting. **$12.95**

407-80 ALTERNATIVE APPROACHES TO EDUCATING YOUNG CHILDREN. Martha Abbott, Ph.D.; Brenda Galina, Ph.D.; Robert Granger, Ph.D., Barry Klein, Ph.D. Delves into the theoretical basis behind three major programmatic approaches to education: programs emphasizing skill development; cognitive growth; and affective development. This book encourages the reader to develop his or her own theoretical and philosophical position. Each approach is discussed according to rationale and Philosophy, Curriculum Goals, Planning of Instruction, Use of Physical Space, Instructional Materials, Evaluation Methods, and the Instructional Role of the Teacher and Child. **$6.95**

413-80 YOUNG CHILDREN'S BEHAVIOR. Johanne Peck, Ph.D. Approaches to discipline and guidance to help the readers deal more effectively with young children. Six units focus on "Examining Your Goals," "Looking At Behavior," "Young Children's Views of Right, Wrong and Rules," "Applying Behavior Modification," and "Supporting Childs Needs." **$7.95**

406-80 THE WHOLE TEACHER. Kathy R. Thornburg, Ph.D. Designed for education majors and teachers of early childhood programs, this book presents a unified approach to teacher training. Topics addressed include: personal attites, curriculum planning and development; classroom management techniques; working with volunteers, staff and parents; and professional development.

418-80 ORIENTATION TO PRE-SCHOOL ASSESSMENT. T. Thomas McMurrain. Designed for the child development center staff, this handbook presents a clear description of the effective assessment of the individual child. In addition, this manual is the user's guide to HUMANICS CHILD DEVELOPMENT ASSESSMENT FORM, a developmental checklist of skills and behavior that normally emerge during the 3 to 6 year range. Includes 5 assessment tools. **$14.95**

419A-80 COMPETENCIES: A SELF STUDY GUIDE FOR TEACHING COMPETENCIES IN EARLY CHILDHOOD. Mary E. Kasindorf. Divided into six competency areas and thirteen functional areas of competence as identified by the Child Development Consortium. This guide can be used to identify existing teaching skills and training needs. Designed to serve as an aid for those preparing for the C.D.A. credital. It contains checklists of teacher and child behaviors and activities that would indicate competence and can be used in assembling a C.D.A. portfolio. **$12.95**

humanics

Post Office Box 7447
Atlanta, Georgia 30309

PROJECT IDEAS

416-80 AEROSPACE PROJECTS FOR YOUNG CHILDREN. Jane Caballero, Ph.D. This "first of it's kind" manual provides teachers and young students with an overview of aerospace history from kites and balloons, on to helicopters, gliders and airplanes, through todays satellites and the space shuttle. Each chapter is followed by interdisciplinary activities and field trip suggestions. **$12.95**

403-80 MATH MAGIC. Filled with ideas for creating a stimulating pre-school learning environment, this book encourages active participation in the learning process. Through songs, limericks, puzzles, games, and personal involvement it will help children become accustomed to basic math principles, such as classification, seriation, the development of logical thinking, as well as teaching them basic problem solving skills. Comes with "Magic Pouch" which contains full size games, puzzles, bulletin board aids and whimsical animals (17 x 24) as a supplement to the text. **$12.95**

Vol. I, 409-80, Vol. II, 410-80. WHEN I GROW UP. Michele Kavanaugh, Ph.D. Provides activities for expanding the human potential of male and female students, while eliminating sex-role stereotypes. Volume I contains experiences for pre-kindergarten thru 8th grade students. Volume II continues with input suitable for high school through young adulthood.
$10.95 ea.

408-80 METRIC MAGIC. Kathy R. Thornburg, Ph.D. and James L. Thornburg, Ph.D. A fun book of creative classroom activities, *Metric Magic* was developed to teach preschoolers through sixth graders to think "metric." Includes action oriented activities involving the concept of length and progress through mass, area, volume, capacity, time, speed, and temperature. **$8.95**

417-80 ART PROJECTS FOR YOUNG CHILDREN. Jane Caballero, Ph.D. Over 100 stimulating projects for pre-school and elementary age children, including: drawing; painting; cut and paste; flannel and bulletin boards; puppets; clay; printing; textiles; and photography. Designed for those with limited budget and time schedule. Success oriented. $12.95

400-A CHILD'S PLAY. Barbara Trencher, M.S. A fun-filled activities and material book which goes from puppets and mobiles to poetry and songs, to creatively fill the pre-schoolers day. This handbook is a natural addition to a CDA or other competency-based learning program and has been used nation-wide for this purpose. $12.95

415-80 DESIGNING EDUCATIONAL MATERIALS FOR YOUNG CHILDREN. Jane Cabellero, Ph.D. A competency based approach providing over 125 illustrated activities encompassing language arts, health and safety, puppetry, math, and communication skills. Suggested functional areas and stated purpose for each activity make this a valuable tool for the CDA candidate. $14.95

PARENT INVOLVEMENT

419-80 FAMILY ENRICHMENT TRAINING. Gary Wilson and T. Thomas McMurrain. Designed for a workshop of six sessions, this program focuses on concerns for families today including communication, family relations, discipline, and developing self-esteem. Techniques such as role playing, small and large group interaction, and journals encourage participants to develop greater understanding of themselves and others. This package includes a manual for trainers, a participants "log" and the booklet "Dialog for Parents." $12.95

102-80 PARENTS AND TEACHERS. Gary B. Wilson. Offers strategies for staff trainers or anyone involved in parent or adult education. Included are training techniques which facilitate group interaction, team building, effective communication and self awareness. Designed to build a program promoting increased parent-staff interaction, each activity includes clear instructions, stated objectives, lists of materials and time requirements. $12.95

106-80 WORKING TOGETHER. Anthony J. Colleta, Ph.D. This practical handbook includes: plans for parent participation in the classroom; alternative approaches to teaching parenting skills; ideas for home based activities; and supplements to parent programs in the form of child development guides and checklists. $12.95

107-80 WORKING PARENTS. Susan Brown and Pat Kornhauser. Designed to make a positive impact on the family life of working parents, this book presents techniques which promote constructive and enjoyable parent-child interaction without disrupting the families daily routine. $12.95

24 Hour Direct Mail Service:
404-874-2176

420-80 BUILDING SUCCESSFUL PARENT-TEACHER PARTNERSHIPS. Kevin J. Swick, Ph.D., Carol F. Hobson, Ph.D. and R. Eleanor Duff, Ph.D. Deals with the issues of parent involvement by including: an in depth examination of the changing nature of parenting and teaching in recent decades – the emergence of the two-parent working family, the vanishing extended family, the one-parent working family, and a comprehensive plan for implementing successful parent-teacher programs. $10.00

ASSESSMENT

CD-507 CABS – CHILDREN ADAPTIVE SCALE. Bert O. Richmond and Richard H. Kicklighter. A testing tool for children ages 5-10 years. Created to measure skills in the following areas: (1) language development; (2) independent functioning; (3) family role performance; (4) economic-vocational activity and (5) socialization. Useful for enabling teachers to plan remediation for the child's level of adaptive behavior. Designed to be administered directly to the child.
Manual $14.95   Student Test Booklet $.65 ea.

ADOLESCENTS

411A-80 I LIVE HERE, TOO. Wanda Grey. Designed for the teacher who would like to improve the atmosphere in the classroom by helping each student to develop a more positive self concept. Themes such as "You Are One Of A Kind," "Know How You Feel," "You And Other People," "As Others See You," and "Using Your Creativity," will foster in children a better understanding of themselves and the people around them. $8.95

414S-80 H.E.L.P. FOR THE ADOLESCENT. Norma Banas, M.Ed. and J. H. Wills, M.S. Explores the underlying causes of the problems of the high school underachiever or potential dropout. Useful tests, programs and reading references are included to help identify "learning weaknesses" and promote "learning strengths." $6.95

humanics
Post Office Box 7447
Atlanta, Georgia 30309

SOCIAL SERVICES

302-80 ASSESSING STAFF DEVELOPMENT NEEDS. Gary B. Wilson, Gerald Pavloff and Larry Linkes. Provides a step-by-step methodology for determining the training needs of child development programs and planning their resolution. Tear-out worksheets and staff questionnaires will help clarify job descriptions and goal definitions, in conjunction with the needs assessment. $3.00

206-80 A SYSTEM FOR RECORD KEEPING. Gary B. Wilson, T. Thomas McMurrain and Barbara Trencher. Designed for family oriented social service agencies. This handbook is an integral part of HUMANICS Record Keeping System and should be used as a guide to proper use of the HUMANICS Record Keeping Forms. $12.95

201-80 INTERVENTION IN HUMAN CRISIS. T. Thomas McMurrain, Ph.D. Clearly presented intervention strategies based on an evaluation of crisis intensity and the response capacity of the individual or family. Rights, risks and responsibilities of the helper are also discussed. $6.95

MAINSTREAMING

404S-80 NEW APPROACHES TO SUCCESS IN THE CLASSROOM. Norma Banas, M.Ed. and J. A. Wills, M.S. A companion volume to Identifying Early Learning Gaps, designed for mainstream children in kindergarten through third grade. Includes activities structured to inspire the student who has experienced repeated failure and to help him or her acquire learning skills in the areas of reading, writing and arithmetic. Can be used in the classroom for the entire group or for a small group. $12.95

412S-80 LATON: THE PARENT BOOK. Mary Tom Riley, Ed.D. Presents a training plan for parents of handicapped children, designed to acquaint them with the resources, facilities, educational opportunities and diagnostic processes available to help them raise their children. This easy to read book will encourage parents to get involved. $12.95

New Publications

REALTALK: EXERCISES IN FRIENDSHIP AND HELPING SKILLS. George M. Gazda, Ed.D., William C. Childers, Ph.D., Richard P. Walters, Ph. D. A human relations training program for secondary school students including student text and instructor manual. REALTALK includes training in getting along with others, making and keeping friends, leadership, helping others deal with their problems, and learning how to talk with practically anyone about practically anything.

THE LOLLYPOP TEST: A DIAGNOSTIC SCREENING TEST OF SCHOOL READINESS. Alex L. Chew, Ed.D. A lollypop loved by all. Children will enjoy taking this test for school readiness, educators will appreciate the easy quick, and significant results. Purpose of the test: (1) to assist the schools in identifying children needing additional readiness activities before entering first grade (2) to identify children with special problems and (3) to assist schools in planning individual and group instructional objectives. Culture-Free.

SPECIAL INTRODUCTORY PRICE $14.95 each

ORDER FORM

ORDER NO.	TITLE/DESCRIPTION	QUANTITY	PRICE

Subtotal . . . .

Ga. residents
add 4% sales tax . . . . .

Add shipping and
handling charges . . . . .

TOTAL . . . .

humanics

Make checks payable to:

HUMANICS LIMITED
P. O. Box 7447
Atlanta, Georgia 30309

Ship to:

NAME _____

ORGANIZATION _____

ADDRESS _____

CITY_____ STATE_____ ZIP_____

_____
(AREA CODE) TELEPHONE NO.

Institutional P.O. No._____

Date _____

Shipping and Handling Charges

Up to $10.00 add	$1.25
$10.01 to $20.00 add	$2.25
$20.01 to $40.00 add	$3.25
$40.01 to $70.00 add	$4.25
$70.01 to $100.00 add	$5.25
$100.01 to $125.00 add	$6.25
$125.01 to $150.00 add	$7.25
$150.01 to $175.00 add	$8.25
$175.01 to $200.00 add	$9.25

Orders over $200. vary depending
on method of shipment.